BASIC ACCOUNTING
FOR THE SMALL BUSINESS

BASIC ACCOUNTING FOR THE SMALL BUSINESS

Simple, foolproof techniques for keeping your books straight and staying out of trouble

Clive G. Cornish, C.G.A.

Self-Counsel Press
(a division of)
International Self-Counsel Press Ltd.
Canada   U.S.A.

Printed in Canada

First edition: January 1972
Second edition: June 1973
Third edition: March 1974
Fourth edition: July 1976
Fifth edition: April 1979
Sixth edition: August 1983
Seventh edition: August 1987
Eighth edition: September 1990
Ninth edition: March 1992;
Reprinted: February 1993; April 1994; August 1995; February 1997

Canadian Cataloguing in Publication Data
    Cornish, Clive G., date—
        Basic accounting for the small business

        (Self-counsel business series)
        First ed. published as: Our accountant's guide to running a small business. 1972. Fifth ed. published as: Our accountant's guide for the small business. 1979.
        ISBN 0-88908-998-1

        1. Small business—Accounting.   I.Title.   II. Series.
HF5635.C67 1992   657'.9042   C92-091167-6

Self-Counsel Press
(a division of)
International Self-Counsel Press Ltd.
Head and Editorial Office
1481 Charlotte Road
North Vancouver, British Columbia V7J lHl
U.S. Address
1704 N. State Street
Bellingham, Washington 98225

CONTENTS

SAMPLES

NOTICE TO READERS

In this book, the accountant is consistently referred to as "he." This is for readability only and is not intended in any way to disparage the growing number of talented women who now grace the ranks of the accounting profession.

To save space and to increase legibility, the cents column has been omitted in many of the samples. Where a percentage calculation would have produced a fraction, the amount has been rounded to the nearest dollar.

1

YOUR ACCOUNTANT

This book is chock-full of references to "your accountant." It would be a lot fuller if the author hadn't gone through the manuscript with a blue pencil and scored out the phrase about a hundred times.

So it might be a good idea, before going further, to stop and ask, "What is an accountant?"

There is no pat answer to the question, principally because accountants themselves cannot agree on the subject. Bookkeepers, for instance, like to be called accountants, and accountants like to be called auditors. (Auditors would like to be called "Your Excellency," but they are too modest to insist on it.)

Sometimes you can tell these people apart by the language they speak, although not always. A bookkeeper tells you he will figure out your income tax, an accountant says he will calculate it, whereas an auditor feels positively unhappy unless he can compute it.

Some accountants have professional degrees, others do not. An accountant without a degree may well be a topnotch accountant — but he has to blow his own trumpet. The man with a degree doesn't have to, because he has a set of initials after his name that speak for him.

No matter what your friend may call himself — C.A., C.G.A., Accountant and Auditor, Income Tax Specialist, or whatever — if he is in public practice — that is to say, if his services are available to anyone who will pay for them — then he is the man referred to in this manual as "your accountant."

He is the man who writes up your books, once a week, once a month, or once a year, and at the proper time he makes up your income tax return.

How much work he does (and, consequently, the amount of his fee) depends largely on you.

Your accountant doesn't particularly like bookkeeping, because it gets monotonous, day in and day out. Still less does he like what you might call "pre-bookkeeping," which is work that should really be done by you or an employee.

However, he will do anything that is necessary to keep your books in good shape, and whether it is pre-bookkeeping work or highly skilled statement and tax work, he will base the charge for his services on the time it takes.

For this reason it will pay you to do as much of the preliminary work as you can. And, although it may seem strange, your accountant will prefer less work and a lower fee, rather than all your work and a higher fee.

There are several reasons for this attitude.

First, a good public accountant is always pressed for time. I don't know why this is, and it is all the more peculiar when you consider he is always willing to take on another client. Nevertheless, it is true, and consequently anything that permits him to devote less time to a client's books and still do a good job is welcome.

Second, accounting takes considerable professional skill, whereas bookkeeping takes less, and pre-bookkeeping almost none. Your accountant works best when he can exercise his top skill, and consequently if you relieve him of routine work, he will do a better job of straight accounting.

Third, your accountant hopes that your business will eventually grow to the point where you have your own full-time accountant, because then he will become your auditor (with fees at a higher rate per hour).

Of course, not all public accountants think along the above lines — but most do. And even if your accountant is a friend who does accounting in his spare time, the chances are that he carries around with him a mental picture of the day he can quit his job and start an accounting practice of his own.

a. WHEN AND WHERE DOES AN ACCOUNTANT WORK?

Some accountants will pick up your books and take them to their own offices to work on, while some will write up the books in your place of business. Still others will expect you to deliver your books and papers to their offices and then pick them up a few days later when ready.

You can make your own arrangements, but remember this: your accountant's time is your money.

Accountants themselves usually prefer you to pick up and deliver, and unless they are unexpectedly not busy, they prefer to work in their own offices.

You may enjoy having someone to talk to in the store or shop, but your accountant will be wriggling in his chair, trying to get the work done and at the same time contribute an occasional remark so you won't think he's discourteous. He would sooner be in his own office where he can work without distraction and use mechanical aids such as adding machines and calculators.

Your books should be written up regularly. This can be anything from once a month to once a year.

Once a week is too often. It means your accountant is doing work you should do, such as making up weekly pay cheques or even typing your invoices.

Of course, if you are prepared to pay accounting fees for straight clerical work, that's all right. But the chances are you would be further ahead if you paid somebody part-time wages to do your pre-bookkeeping chores. The fact is that the main accounting entries come up only once a month, so that if your accountant works on your books more often, he cannot help but waste a certain amount of time.

If you don't require monthly statements or monthly sales-tax returns, you may find a two- or three-month write-up satisfactory. It might even reduce your accounting costs, although not by very much.

You can even let your books go for a whole year without having them written up and often it works out very nicely. But if you do this you will find that no matter how many details you write down, there are always others you carry in your head and in a year you will forget some of them.

Every accountant has gone through the business of waiting patiently while his client broods over a cancelled cheque and mutters, "who is Joe Smithers and why did I pay him $50?"

Another disadvantage of the once-a-year write-up is that it is often a rush job, usually to beat the income tax deadline, and that means your accountant will cut corners, omitting to ask you for information when perhaps he should.

b. PROVIDE YOUR ACCOUNTANT WITH ALL NECESSARY INFORMATION

You should make it a rule not to hide anything from your accountant. You may think you are hiding something, but you can be pretty sure he knows about it even if he doesn't let on. No one can be a public accountant for long without running up against all the standard dodges and a good many more besides.

To be truthful, your accountant is not overly concerned about your business morals. He will take the information you furnish him and write up the books accordingly. If you are deliberately not reporting all your sales, he won't reproach you, although he may think less of you.

He doesn't guarantee the correctness of your financial statements. He is not auditing your books, so he does not have to state that, in his opinion, they are correct.

He knows the statements reflect the information you supplied and that you are the person who signs your income tax return.

However, he would prefer to see you do what 99% of his clients do, namely, put everything in the open and hide nothing.

From a tax point of view he will give you all the breaks his professional mind can think up. From an accounting point of view he will give you value for your money.

He is usually a quiet sort of chap, otherwise he wouldn't be an accountant. He would be out selling cars or real estate and making a lot more money than he'll ever make as an accountant.

He has his standards of professional integrity and they are high. He can be a good friend of yours if you will meet him half way.

2

ON BUYING A BUSINESS

You talked it over with your family and with any friends who would stop to listen; you littered the kitchen table with figures scribbled on bits of paper and you did mental arithmetic until you were nearly dizzy; and any way you looked at it, it still looked good to you.

True, your brother-in-law muttered something about "throwing up a good steady job," and talked about "rolling stones gathering no moss," but you had already made up your mind. You sniffed the heady air of independence and you were through with working for a boss. Why, in a few years from now...!

So — you borrowed on your insurance, sold your bonds, haggled a bit over the down payment, but finally gave the previous owner pretty close to what he was asking. Very likely he was selling out "for reasons of health," and still more likely, as soon as your cheque has cleared, he will suddenly get well and buy a business from another party, who also happens to be selling out "for reasons of health," etc.

However, that is by the way. You have paid your money and you are now the owner of a business. Don't forget, though, unless it was an all-cash deal, you are also on the paying end of an impressive agreement for sale, chattel mortgage, or whatever other type of encumbrance the lawyers have thought up.

Don't mislay this document. On the other hand, don't put it away in your safe deposit box because it is the first thing your accountant will want to see when he sets up your books.

In the meantime, let's have a look at it and see if, as sometimes happens, the lawyers have been so smart that, from an accounting point of view, they have pleasantly gummed up the works.

In the first place, you may think that all you have done is buy a business.

Your accountant will think differently. He will maintain, quite correctly, that you have acquired a group of assets (meaning *things*), and that you have assumed a liability (meaning *debt*).

The assets may include any or all of the following:
Merchandise
Accounts receivable
Furniture and fixtures
Equipment and machinery
Cars and trucks
Buildings
Land
Goodwill

There are two ways to draw up an agreement for sale. The preferable way would be to itemize the assets, like this:

Land	$ 6 000.00
Buildings	24 000.00
Merchandise	13 852.00
1½ ton truck	3 600.00
1 Showcase	1 400.00
1 Counter scales	600.00
Goodwill	10 548.00
	$60 000.00

Few people take the time and trouble to see that an itemized list gets into the body of the agreement. The merchandise inventory may have been inserted at the figure agreed on, but the chances are the rest of the purchase price covers a hodgepodge such as this:

"...Lot 26, Block 14, in the City of Blank, and all buildings, situate thereon, together will all fixtures and appurtenances heretofore known as the Jones Pickle Works, and for the sum of $60 000.00, payable, etc..."

This happens because everybody is in a hurry. The seller wants to get his or her money, you want to get the business rolling, and the lawyer wants to get back to an important brief he or she is working on. Accounting details can be worried about later. That is the general thought — and "worried" is precisely the word to use.

a. WHAT YOU GOT FOR YOUR MONEY

If your agreement has been drawn up in the hodgepodge style, it is now up to you to figure out a set of values to account for the purchase price. This is not hard if you do it step by step, but there are pitfalls, so let's go over the items which may cause trouble.

Land and buildings: If these are lumped together you are going to have to split the amount into two figures. The reason is depreciation (meaning *annual write-off*). For income tax purposes you may claim depreciation on your building, but not on land.

One way to split the total is to get hold of a copy of last year's local tax assessment. This will have on it two figures, one for "land" and the other for "improvements." The total of the two will probably be less than the true value of the property (for which you should be thankful, as otherwise your taxes would be higher), but you can make good use of the ratio.

Thus, suppose your local assessment shows:

Land	$ 4 000.00
Improvements	16 000.00
Total	$20 000.00

The ratio of land to improvements is 1 to 4. If, then, the actual value of the land and buildings is $30 000.00 you can split this figure in the 1-to-4 ratio and get:

$ 6 000.00 for the cost of your land

  24 000.00 for the cost of your building

$30 000.00 Total actual value

If you don't like the ratio on the tax assessment notice, you can use your own. Using the tax ratio, though, gives you this advantage: if you ever get into an argument with the tax department over asset values, you can show that they are based on an impartial, outside opinion.

Cars and trucks: You should be able to make a good guess at these values. Consult the newspaper classified columns if you are in doubt.

Furniture and fixtures: Within reason, you can set your own valuation and nobody will dispute it.

Equipment and machinery: Again, within reason, you can set your own figures.

Merchandise inventory: This item deserves more attention than it usually gets. If the previous owner took stock and can produce his inventory sheets, use that total. If, on the other hand, he or she has only a hazy idea ("Oh, around $14 000.00, I guess"), it will pay you to take stock yourself. You may have to estimate the cost of some of the stuff, but that's all right. You'll end up with a fair idea of what you have and what it's worth. Without this information you are going to be up a tree when you try to figure out how much profit you've made.

Goodwill: This is the most contentious item of all. To begin with, what is goodwill?

An accounting textbook might define it thus: "The capitalization of excess earning power attributable to business connections, trade reputation and customer buying habits."

A simpler definition would be: "The premium you pay for getting what you want, when you want it."

Goodwill is the spread between the apparent value of the things you bought and the price you paid. If you look back at the example, you'll see that is exactly what happened when you bought the Jones Pickle Works. The things you bought were apparently worth $49 452.00, but you paid (or agreed to pay) $ 60 000.00. The difference of $10 548.00 is for goodwill.

Goodwill, however, does not appear on the books of a business as often as you might think, and the reason is not hard to find. For, whereas you may take a generous tax write-off on your physical assets from year to year, only half of goodwill can be written off, and if you sell your business later the amount written off could go right back into your income.

Therefore, the average buyer of a business, after a little chat with his or her accountant, stands awhile in thought. Then, turning a critical eye on the asset values just figured out, he or she wonders if, after all, the calculations were a little bit on the low side.

You, for instance, have just bought the Pickle Works, and on thinking things over, might decide that the showcase was really worth $1 800.00, and the property, considering the excellent condition of the building, was really worth $40 000.00. Under the combined influence of enlightened self-interest and the tax department, it dawns on you that you have bought assets as follows:

Land	$ 8 000.00
Buildings	32 000.00
Merchandise inventory	13 852.00
1½ ton truck	3 600.00
1 Showcase	1 800.00
1 Counter scales	600.00
Goodwill	148.00
	$60 000.00

This is very nice for you because you can now take an annual write-off on a $32 000.00 building, instead of a $24 000.00 building.

It should be mentioned that the tax department is perfectly familiar with these profound second thoughts, and, in addition, they have in their files complete information on what the building and other assets originally cost. However, they will be reasonable if you will be reasonable. They know that if specific values are not mentioned in your agreement, at least you have paid, or will pay, hard cash for your purchase, and hence your own valuations are backed by something weightier than personal whim.

(Of course, if you and your accountant had carefully worked out values *before* the agreement was drawn up and told your lawyer to put them smack in the middle of the "whereases," *then* you would be in a very strong position to talk back to anybody, including the director of income tax. Because, there, for all the world to see, would be details in black and white, signed and sealed, with no second thoughts.)

Unexpired insurance, prepaid taxes and water rates, etc.: Items of this nature rarely appear on the agreement, but they are always on the "adjustments" sheet that accompanies the deal. Every one of them has its proper place on your books, so make sure your accountant sees the sheet. (And check with the insurance agent to be sure the policies have been endorsed over to you.)

What with one thing and another, it is a good idea to have your accountant sit in or any deal before the papers are made up. Particularly this applies if you are ever tempted to buy an incorporated company.

b. SHOULD YOU BUY SHARES OR ASSETS?

Sometimes it happens that the business you want has been incorporated, and somebody suggests that the simplest thing would be for you to buy the shares.

11

A good rule in one word is: "DON'T!"

FIRST, the company may have all sorts of liabilities hanging over its head, such as income tax, prospective law suits, or just plain debts. It may be that the controlling shareholder honestly doesn't know about these things, or may just have been trying hard to forget them and finally succeeded when you came along.

True, you may obtain a clear-cut guarantee from the seller protecting you ("indemnify and hold harmless" is the way it goes) from any debts that do crop up, but such guarantees can easily turn out to be worthless, and certainly the company's creditors don't give a hoot about them.

SECOND, the corporation may have written down its assets for income tax purposes until they are near zero and can't be written down any more. Whereas, if you buy the *assets* instead of the shares, you can put them on the books at whatever they cost you and enjoy the tax benefits of a healthy write-off.

THIRD, although the company whose shares you propose to buy may have a fat surplus account, you can only draw it out either as salary or dividends, and both will be subject to personal income tax.

Only in special cases, where previous years' losses can be used to offset future taxable profits, should you consider buying shares instead of assets. And if you do encounter such a special case, don't make a move before your accountant has analyzed the whole set-up from start to finish because the tax department also has its own rules about "loss companies."

And now, you are nearly ready to go, but not quite. Very often you and the previous owner hold radically different ideas on store or plant layouts. Or perhaps you had to move into premises that were unsuitable until extensive alterations were made.

The cost of these changes may be heavy and it is not fair to saddle your first year of business with the entire amount (nor is it permissible for income tax purposes). Talk over the situation with your accountant, for he has run into it many times.

If you own the place he may suggest adding the alterations expense to the cost of the building and then writing off a percentage of the whole annually. If you are renting he will set up an "Alterations Account" in your books, and then write it off over the life of your lease.

In any case, let him know what is going on *before* he writes up your books. Otherwise he may charge a lot of costs to "Repairs" or "Supplies" or even "Personal Drawings," and then later have to make corrections.

c. DRIFTING INTO BUSINESS

Many people never do start a business — that is, in the sense that one day they are at leisure and the next day they are in business. They begin with a hobby or some sort of spare-time occupation, pleasurable or otherwise. Gradually they give it more and more time, until the point is reached where more money can be made from spare-time activities than from a full-time job. Or, at any rate, so it seems.

If you started up like this, you are lucky in one way. Your problems have crept up on you, not jumped on you all at once, and you will likely have devised a rule-of-thumb system to take care of them.

There comes a time, however (perhaps the income tax deadline), when the system shows signs of getting out of hand, and your thoughts turn to an accountant.

So you pick out your accountant and the question arises: "What information will he want, and have I got it?"

Basically he will want the information discussed in detail in the first part of this chapter. That is to say, the description of the assets that went into the business, what they cost, or what they are worth, whether they are paid for, and, if not, how much is still owed on them, and to whom.

Note that phrase "what they cost or what they are worth," for therein lies the principal accounting difference between buying a business and drifting into one. When you buy a business the purchase price is a specific amount. The bill of sale may not say how much of the price should go to this or that asset, but you can work out a reasonable set of values for the assets as already outlined.

When you drift into a business, the chances are that the assets you are using have been acquired over a long period of time, and, further, their cost cannot be pinpointed in dollars. Some parts of a machine may have been bought, others received as a gift, or by far the larger part of its value may be due to your own hours of labor. The best thing to do is to make an estimate of "fair market values" as of the date you decide you are running a business and not riding a hobby.

As for the other information your accountant needs, that will depend on how long you have been operating and whether you have reached your business year-end. If your operations have been small and only for a brief period, then you can call in your accountant immediately, and in half an hour's conversation he can obtain all the information he needs.

If you have been operating for some time and your business has been large, then you had best read the chapter on "The Apple-Box Situation" before deciding whether to call your accountant in now, or after you have attended to the preliminaries yourself. (Much will depend on how effective your rule-of-thumb system has proved.)

In any event, don't put off getting an accountant until a week before the income tax deadline. Call him in early, so he can give your business his undivided attention. He can do a better job on your books and his fee will be less.

14

3

SALES

In this country the person who sells the most goods earns the most money.

Whether this is a good thing for the health of the nation, or otherwise, we must leave to those with ability and leisure to ponder the question. But for you it means that sales are the most important part of your business, (even more important than accounting) and, consequently, the way you keep your sales records is also most important.

That is why, for the sake of clarity, you will find this chapter broken up into so many sections, like an act of Parliament, although it will prove more understandable, I hope, than the average act.

a. THE RETAILER

To begin with let us look at the most common of all small businesses — the retail store. This includes groceries, meat markets, variety stores, restaurants, hardware stores, gas stations, millineries, gift shops — in fact, any place where you wait for customers to come to you rather than chase after them.

In all of these businesses the average sale is either small, or else made up of a number of small articles. It is usually for cash, and the proprietors have neither the time nor the inclination to do any more writing than they have to. They want to make sales as rapidly as courtesy permits, and they are interested only in knowing the total dollars taken in.

b. SALES ACROSS THE COUNTER

There may not always be a counter but this is the simplest sale and, therefore, the easiest to describe, so let's get it out of the way.

1. Cash sales

In truth, it is a very simple system. You sell a dollar's worth of goods or services, ring it up or write it down, and that's that.

If you use a cash register, your day's sales will be the total on the register, or (if you have the cumulative type) they will be the difference between the figures at the start of the day and the end of the day. If you don't use a cash register, you will have to use one of the following methods:

(a) Write up each sale on the autographic register and add up the sales slips at the end of the day.

(b) Write down your sales in a book in columns and add up the columns at the end of the day.

(c) Don't write down anything. At the end of the day count the money in the till, allow for any change you put in and the money you paid out, then work back to what must have come in from sales.

The last method is not very satisfactory because you have no check on shortages or overages.

Whatever you do, when you have read the chapter on cash, pick out the cash sheet suited to your needs and use it faithfully.

And now, if you don't sell on credit, you may skip the next bit and jump ahead to "Sales Tax." But if you *do* give credit, plough onwards.

2. Charge sales

Keeping track of charge sales can be a frustrating, time-consuming business, and certainly it has caused many a retail storekeeper to wonder, "Is credit worth giving?"

The basic cause of this distress is the time lag between when the sale is made and when the money — or part of it — is collected. So, here is a temper-saving suggestion.

If your charge sales are small and few, don't consider them as sales until you collect the money.

Of course, you'll have to keep a record somewhere of what your charge customers buy, how much they pay on account, and what they still owe. But for easier bookkeeping, figure your sale as the amount of cash received, *when you receive it.*

Then, at the end of your business year (or at any other time you want a statement), total up the unpaid balances in your charge accounts and give the figure to your accountant so he can make the necessary adjustment on your books.

Did I say, "If your charge sales are small and few?" I should have said, "If you want to save yourself a lot of fuss and bother," for many a not-so-small business uses this method too.

In fact, nearly all old-fashioned (under $1 000) cash registers are designed to facilitate handling charge sales this way. Cash sales and charge account collections (the tape symbols are "Ca." and "Rc." or close variations) are the only figures that are accumulated on the register, so that when you clear it at the end of the day, the total printed is the total cash taken in, and nothing else.

You can put charge sales (symbol: "Ch.") through the machine if you wish, but the amount won't be added in to your register total. You can ring up paid outs (symbol: "Pd.") and the amount won't affect the register total either.

The cash register people design their machines that way because they found out long ago that small merchants prefer to handle charge sales on a "cash basis," despite the fact that bookkeeping texts discuss only the orthodox method, or "accrual basis."

17

However, whether you figure sales on a cash basis (when paid) or on an accrual basis (when made) *provided you have made no mistakes in arithmetic in your charge account books*, either method will give you exactly the same set of figures, as the following comparison shows.

ACCRUAL BASIS (Sales WHEN MADE)

TOTAL ACTUAL SALES FOR THE MONTH	$10 000.00
Subtract: Charge sales included in above	4 000.00
Difference — Straight cash sales	6 000.00
Add: Charge account collections	3 000.00
Total cash taken in during the month	$ 9 000.00

CASH BASIS (Sales WHEN PAID)

Straight cash sales made (and rung up)	$ 6 000.00	
Charge accounts collected (and rung up)	3 000.00	
Total cash taken in during the month		$ 9 000.00
Charge accounts		
Total of balances at start of month	$ 2 500.00	
Total of balances at end of month	$ 3 500.00	
Add: Increase* in charge account balances during the month		$ 1 000.00
TOTAL ACTUAL SALES FOR THE MONTH		$10 000.00

*(If this were a decrease, you would subtract from, and not add to, $9 000.00.)

It must be emphasized that if you make an error in adding up a customer's account, or forget to credit a customer with a payment, you won't know it unless somebody tells you.

18

This is a drawback, but if you are reasonably good at adding and subtracting, it need not be a serious one.

In brief, then, the cash basis for handling charge sales consists in "recognizing" the sale *only when you receive the money*, and in keeping a memo record of sales not paid for and therefore "not recognized."

But to return to orthodox bookkeeping, what should you do if you want to recognize a charge sale at the time it is made?

Ring it up or write it down, just as if it were a cash sale BUT — mark the transaction on your cash register tape with the symbol or code letter provided, or — write or mark "charge" on your autographic register slip so that you'll know it's a charge sale, and not a cash sale.

(a) If you use a cash register

A low-priced machine will not give you a sales total — it will give you only the total of cash received. To get your sales totals you will have to add separately the amounts coded as cash sales and charge sales. To get your "received on account" total (which you will need later) you subtract cash sales from the total cash received.

A more expensive machine will have several registers and you can clear each in turn to give you not only charge and cash sales, but also received-on-account and paid-out totals. This is the kind of machine you will find in large volume retail outlets, where the chore of picking out and adding up different classes of transactions would be too burdensome.

With either type of machine you will need something more informative for your individual charge sales than an amount and a code letter on the tape. This can be anything from a counter-book page to a specially printed sales slip, on which you can write the customer's name and details of the sale. Some cash registers have a slot into which you can insert the sales slip when you ring up a charge sale or a charge account collection. The machine prints the amount and the serial number of the transaction on the slips, thus tying it in with the tape.

But to introduce a note of cheer, electronic cash registers have become not only less expensive but also much more useful. If you can't afford to buy one, try to lease one with an option to buy. The time saved, frustration eliminated and the amount of accurate information obtained make an electronic machine just about the best investment you can make.

(b) If you use an autographic register

You will have to sort out the day's slips into piles, so that you have one for cash sales and another for charge sales, and then add these up separately. You should also add up the slips for charge account collections, as you will need this information.

Frankly, if you have less than 30 sales a day, you don't need a cash register. An autographic register costs a lot less, and with only a part of what you save you can get a small adding machine and still be money ahead. In addition an adding machine is just about the most useful business tool you can have around the place.

To sum up at this point:

— FOR CASH SALES ONLY the daily total is all you need to be concerned with
— FOR CASH SALES PLUS CHARGE SALES ON A CASH BASIS, again, all you need is a daily total
— FOR CASH SALES PLUS CHARGE SALES ON AN ACCRUAL BASIS, you will have three daily figures to work out, namely, your cash sales, your charge sales, and the total of both together.

3. Sales tax

This nuisance was dreamed up by governments in search of money, and it has been so successful that it is likely we will always have it with us. In fact, if you are not yet afflicted with a sales tax, you can be certain that sooner or later you will be.

Among the collection systems used by retailers are:

— PENNY-IN-THE-BOTTLE: exactly what it sounds like, tax cash into a bottle, sales cash into the till.

— TICKETS: you tear them off a pre-numbered roll as each sale is made. The rolls come in one, two, and five cent denominations. At the end of the day from the serial numbers of the tickets unused, you figure out how many tickets you tore off, and from that how much tax you collected.

— YOUR CASH REGISTER: this applies only if you have a multiple register machine.

— A PIECE OF RULED PAPER: one column for tax, another for net sales.

— A STRAIGHT PERCENTAGE OF SALES: this is fine when everything is taxable, and taxable at the same rate; otherwise, no.

All of the above methods work, and all of them are nuisances.

As a general rule it makes for easier figuring if you can treat your total income, tax and all, as your gross sales figure, and then work back to arrive at net sales and tax.

There is one tricky little complication about sales tax that you should keep in mind. If, for example, your tax rate is 3%, and your gross sales for the day, *including tax*, are $100.00, then the tax payable is not $3.00. It is 3/103 of $100.00, or $2.91.

The same calculation applies if you sell anything "GST included." Thus, on a sale of $100.00 GST included, the real selling price is $93.45 and the GST is $6.55, or 7/107 of $100.00. Incidentally, if selling "GST included" becomes your standard policy you are legally required to put up conspicuous signs to that effect.

If you are billing a customer with GST-included price and if that customer is a GST registrant, then you are required to disclose the amount of the GST elsewhere on the invoice. This is so that your customer will be able to claim the correct amount as a GST tax input credit.

The most important thing about sales tax is to keep a record of the amount you will have to send in, whether or not you collect it at that time. Sales tax on large substantial sales (say, $100 or more) is easier to handle because detailed written records of large transactions are necessary and rarely mislaid. The penny-by-penny tax is the real nuisance, particularly when some sales are exempt from tax.

If your sales are mainly of the large, substantial type, then you won't need a cash register. Instead, you will have to make a list of your sales and the tax collected. You cannot run your business without knowing what your sales are, nor is it wise to send in sales tax without keeping some evidence of how much was collected and when. Large sales, however, require different treatment from small sales, so let us consider them separately.

4. Goods and services tax

On January 1, 1991, the federal government introduced a 7% tax on all "goods and services," with the exception of most food, medical expenses, and certain other items which were deemed basic necessities. This tax, known as the GST, is in addition to existing provincial sales taxes and, in some cases may result in tax on tax.

The GST replaces the federal sales tax and is designed strictly as a tax to be paid by the consumer. This means the ultimate buyer, your customer, pays the 7% and not you. To ensure that this takes place you apply for a refund of all the 7% tax your business may have paid during the current reporting period. This refunding is done by means of an "input tax credit," or all the amounts that you have already paid during the same period.

The system is very broad based. Taxwise, if you paid out more than you took in, you will get the excess back from the government. This is not as odd as it sounds, because it assumes that sooner or later you will sell merchandise on which you paid tax, and at that point Revenue Canada will get its money back.

To comply with the GST regulations, some extra book-keeping is required, but fortunately not very much. The nuts and bolts of the extra procedures are set out in chapters 4 and 5.

If your total sales are less than $30 000 a year you are not obliged to register or file periodic reports. You are thus saved the time and cost of collecting and remitting GST. However, any GST you pay when you buy supplies for your business cannot be claimed back from the government.

If your total sales are more than $30 000 a year you must register and file periodic reports as required by the regulations. However, if your business falls within broad classifications, and depending on the volume, you may have the option of disregarding your analysis of taxable and non-taxable sales. You will still collect the GST when called for, but instead of deducting "input tax credits" when remitting tax, you will pay a flat percentage of total sales, ranging from 1% to 5%, depending on the classification into which you fit. This choice is not a step to be taken lightly, and I suggest you defer any decision until you have discussed it with your accountant.

There are many publications available to guide you through the complexities of the GST and one of the best is put out by the people who publish this book.

c. SALES IN THE MAIL

1. Invoices

There are many businesses in which every transaction is preceded by a polite form of haggling known as "sales talk" so that when the deal is wound up, both parties feel that something noteworthy has been accomplished. You think your customer is entitled to something more formal than a page from a counter-book, so you type out an invoice in triplicate. Let's say the wording is:

To one only, Model B, semi-automatic junketizer, with hand-operated directional fin, (Catalogue No. 73474)	$727.00
Installation (labor)	75.00
10 gals. (45.5 litres) special cylinder oil	52.00
Prepaid freight charges	65.00
	$919.00
GST	64.33
	$983.33

We will presume your invoices are pre-numbered consecutively by the printer and padded in batches of 25 or 50. We can presume, also, that if you left it to the printer, he or she could put the invoice numbers somewhere up in the right-hand corner — but you didn't leave it to the printer. You specifically stated that the numbers be put in the *lower* right-hand corner. (This is a small thing, but when you leaf through invoices looking for one particular number, as you will sooner or later, it will save time and energy.)

And still on the subject of pre-numbered invoices, *never* destroy a cancelled or botched invoice. Put your file copy in the proper order and leave it there. Then, six months later, you won't get insomnia wondering if the missing number represents an unpaid invoice.

But, to return to the invoice you have just typed out, basically this is a sales slip in formal dress. For this very reason it deserves full dress treatment, which consists of writing down the details in a book called a "Sales Journal."

A sample is worth more than a sales talk, so if you will look at Sample #1 you can examine a typical sales journal page. Notice the figures are spread *across* the page, and not downward as they are on the invoice.

24

SAMPLE #1
SALES JOURNAL

Date	Name	Invoice number	Received cash from customer	Charged customer	NET SALES	Provincial sales tax payable	GST payable	Cartage charged	Installa- tion charged	Cylinder oil charged	Prepaid freight charged	Memo
2	C. Breen	463	983		727		64		75	52	65	P.T. exempt
3	J. Osman	464	128		100	5	8	15				
3	P. Spellman	465		135	120	6	9					
4	J. Woodward	466		27	20	1	2	4				
5	Delta Company	467		549	460		32	22	35			P.T. exempt
6	R. Dixon	468		241	200	10	15	6				
JANUARY TOTALS			1 471	7 198	6 992	106	560	157	322	168	364	

You don't have to use a column for each item on the invoice. You could put just the invoice total in the sales column and let it go at that. Most people, however, like to have the details spread out, particularly the sales tax, which has to be put down somewhere.

You'll notice, too, that the total of each invoice is actually written down twice. Once, under either "Received cash," or "Charged customer," and again as the sum of the figures under "Net sales," "Provincial sales tax," "GST," "Cartage," etc., across the page. This is done for an important reason.

Just as all the various charges that go into a single invoice should add up correctly to the invoice amount, so all the *column totals* of charges should add up correctly to the *column totals* of the invoice amounts. Like this:

Cash received column	$1 471.00
Charge customers	7 198.00
	$8 669.00
Net sales column	$6 992.00
Sales tax column	106.00
GST column	560.00
Cartage column	157.00
Installation charge	322.00
Cylinder oil supplied	168.00
Freight prepaid	364.00
	$8,669.00

If the column totals don't balance, it means somewhere you have made a mistake in addition, either on an invoice or in a column, and it should be located right away.

The column headings in Sample #1 are in plain English. You should make a note, though, of their accounting equivalents, because you are going to encounter them continually as you go along. Here they are:

English	Accounting Equivalent
Received cash from customer	Dr. Cash
Charged customer	Dr. Accounts receivable
Sales tax, payable on taxable sales	Cr. Sales tax
Cartage passed on to customer	Cr. Cartage
Installation charge	
passed on to customer	Cr. Installation charges

"Dr." stands for "Debit" and "Cr." stands for "Credit," which are standard abbreviations in accounting, as is "A/c" for "Account" or "Accounts."

2. Trade-in allowances

If you sell durable goods (i.e., something that won't fall apart before six months) you are going to be plagued with the trade-in problem. Fundamentally, a trade-in deal is nothing more than a sale, followed immediately by a purchase, and that's the way to record it.

If, for instance, you sell a late model junketizer for $600, and allow $400 on a last year's machine, forgetting about tax, cartage, etc., for the moment, the way it goes on your books is this:

Dr. Cash (or Accounts receivable)	$600.00	
Cr. Sales		$600.00
Dr. Purchases	400.00	
Cr. Cash (or Accounts receivable)		400.00

Or, if you prefer, you can condense it like this:

Dr. Cash (or Accounts receivable)	$200.00	
Dr. Purchases	400.00	
Cr. Sales		$600.00

Whatever you do, don't over condense it like this:

Dr. Cash (or Accounts receivable)	$200.00	
Cr. Sales		$200.00

because that isn't what happened. If you did that you would distort your cost-to-sales ratio and also throw out your sales tax calculations if any.

27

3. Refunds and returns

If you are doing a sales-across-the-counter business, you can treat refunds and returns as if they were an expense. There is a place for them on your cash sheet, described fully in the next chapter. If your business is the sales-in-the-mail type, an entry must go in your sales journal, and there are two ways of making it.

The first is like this:

Alongside every column in your journal you put a "reverse" column. That's to say:

> — next to "Sales" put "Refunds and returns" (Dr. Sales returns)
> — next to "Received cash" put "Cash paid out" (Cr. Cash)
> — next to "Customer charged" put "Customer credited" (Cr.A/c receivable)
> — next to "Tax collected" put "Tax refunded" (Dr. Sales tax)

and so on. Then, when you issue a credit note to a customer, you again spread the figures across the page, but this time in the reverse columns. Take a look at Sample #2.

The second method is simpler, although it won't give you the monthly total of your returns. It's like this:

Write the credit figures in the same columns as the sales figures but use *red* ink or *red* pencil.

Red figures in bookkeeping are the universal signal for "the opposite of normal." So, when you add your columns at the end of the month, *subtract* the red figures from the black. You will then have corrected net totals for the month.

In Sample #3, due to the limitations of the printing press, the red figures aren't shown in red. They are, however, in parentheses.

Now let's sum up what you have achieved with your sales journal. You have —

(a) arranged your figures so that the addition of the columns will give daily, weekly, or monthly totals (depending on your chop-off point) for sales, sales tax, cash sales, charge sales, cartage, installation, and what not. In short, a summary of your business activity),

(b) completed a piece of work that your accountant would do, and charge you for, if you didn't do it,

(c) taken a real step toward understanding the books.

4. Special cases

Departmentalization This is a luxury you may profitably indulge in if the information it yields is worth the extra work it entails. Thus, if you are running a restaurant and sell tobacco as a sideline, your gross profit percentage on food will be (or should be) several times the percentage for tobacco, and if you lump all sales together you will have a mixed percentage figure of no particular value. Whereas if you keep sales (*and purchases*) of food and tobacco separate, then if the tobacco percentage drops to zero, you may reasonably suppose that someone is lifting cigarettes behind your back.

If may be that you have several salespeople working for you and you want to know how much each is selling either for comparison or for figuring out commissions. Departmentalize your sales (a column in the sales journal for each kind of sale) and the information is there when you want it. As a general rule, a small business doesn't need departments and a large business can't do without them. As you grow from one to the other, you can decide when departmental information is worth the work involved in obtaining it.

SAMPLE #2
SALES JOURNAL
("Reverse" columns)

Date	Detail	Invoice #	Sundry charge backs	Sundry credits	Cash		Customers		Returns and refunds	Sales	Provincial sales tax		GST	
					Rec'd	Paid out	Chg.	Credit.			Returns/refunds	Chg.	Paid	Collected
2	P. Spengle	863			90					80		4		6
5	F. Nixon	864					224			200		10		14
5	T. Squires (Prov. tax exempt)	865		26			100			93				7
6	R. Garson (Cr. Prepd. Frght. Cr. Installation)	866		40			317			220		11		20
7	F. Nixon (Credit note)	867						22	20		1		1	
8	K. Weaver (Cr. Prepd. Frght.)	868		12			125			100		5		8
9	P. Spengle	869				22			20		1		1	
12	N. Powers	870			45					40		2		3
14	R. Garson (Credit note) (Dr. Installation)	871	20					21					1	
16	L. Squibb (Cr. Cartage) (Cr. Installation)	872		27 38			338			240		12		21
16	K. Weaver (Dr. Prepd. Frght.)	873	2					24	20		1		1	
	JANUARY TOTALS		98	357	321	81	2 503	179	132	2 151	8	96	9	207

30

NOTES ON SAMPLE #2

Note that cartage, installation, and prepaid freight charged out are grouped in "Sundry chargebacks." This is because two columns for each item would make the page so wide as to be unwieldy. It is bad enough as it is, which is why the second method (Sample #3) is usually preferred.

In the above example:

— on the 7th, F. Nixon was given a credit note for returning part of the goods he bought on the 5th

— on the 9th, P. Spengle got a cash refund for returning part of the goods he bought on the 2nd.

— on the 14th, R. Garson complained that your man took twice as long as he should have when he installed the equipment bought on the 6th. You knuckled under and gave him a credit note.

— on the 16th, K. Weaver returned some of the goods you included by mistake in his order of the 8th. Accordingly, you issued a credit note for part of the original freight bill.

A pretty thin month for the business, but it serves to illustrate the "reverse column" type of sales journal.

SAMPLE #3
SALES JOURNAL
(Condensed)

Date	Detail	Invoice #	Dr. Cash	Dr. A/c Receivable	Cr. Sales	Cr. Prov. Sales tax	Cr. GST	Cr. Installation	Cr. Prepd Freight	Cr. Cartage
2	P. Spengle	863	90		80	4	6			
5	F. Nixon	864		224	200	10	14			
5	T. Squires (Prov. tax exempt)	865		100	93		7			
6	R. Garson	866						40	26	
7	F. Nixon (Credit note)	867		(22)	(20)	(1)	(1)			
8	K. Weaver	868		125	100	5	8		12	
9	P. Spengle	869	(22)		(20)	(1)	(1)			
12	N. Powers	870	45		40	2	3			
14	R. Garson	871		(21)			(1)	(20)		
16	L. Squibb	872		335	240	12	21	35		27
16	K. Weaver (Returned goods)	873		(24)	(20)	(1)	(1)		(2)	
	JANUARY TOTALS		240	2 181	2 019	88	55	121	63	75

32

NOTES ON SAMPLE #3

This is Sample #2 condensed into single columns.

If you need the information, you may find it handy to have a journal only partly condensed, leaving two columns each for Cash and Accounts Receivable. Thus, instead of showing net cash receipts of $240 as above, you would have "Cash received" $321 and "Cash paid out" $81, as in Sample #2.

For trade-ins (see chapter 3), insert a "Dr. Purchases" column between the invoice number column and the Dr. Cash column.

4

CASH

Long ago, in the days before taxes, recessions, strikes, and other benefits of progress, when you sold someone a pair of shoes you received a sack of wheat, or a pig, or some other useful object in return. It was a very simple system and it worked.

Unfortunately and inevitably, there came along an unemployed accountant who was dissatisfied with simple systems. (He already had five sacks of wheat.) He proposed, and his trusting fellow citizens agreed, that a "medium of exchange" be established.

In the beginning it was cowrie shells, wampum, bright blue beads, or pale yellow metal — it didn't matter much — but from that time on people have had trouble keeping track of money, or, as it is known to accountants, cash.

This is rather a pity, because once you have a cash routine set up, keeping accurate cash records is no more difficult than simple addition and subtraction, and considerably more rewarding.

When I say "rewarding" I mean it literally, for lazy cash records can cause more headaches than all other problems in your business put together. Every public accountant knows of dozens of cases where badly kept, or just plain "unkept," cash records have resulted in double the usual accounting fees.

They have also resulted in numberless instances of overpaid income tax. The owner of the business couldn't prove where the cash came from, so the tax department decided it was from unreported sales and taxed it accordingly. There may have been logical explanations for the money, but the cash records were in such poor shape that the accountant couldn't build a plausible case.

And so, having convinced you, I hope, that if only for self-protection, it is an excellent thing to keep clear, accurate cash records, let us begin by asking, "What is cash?"

The answer, ungrammatical but true, is, "Cash is anything you receive and which you can pay bills with." Cash, therefore, may include any or all of the following:

- currency
- coins
- cheques (other people's)
- money orders
- wholesaler's "deal" coupons
- gas credit card slips
- IOUs

The test of cash is whether it is negotiable. Cabbages would appear correctly as part of your cash receipts, provided you could promptly turn around and pay off a creditor in cabbages.

Certainly all of the items listed above are negotiable. The bank will take the first four, a wholesaler will take coupons, and the tank-truck will take credit slips. As for IOUs if they are yours and you don't redeem them, they become cash withdrawals. If they are somebody else's, they will either be redeemed or will grow up into bad debts, which are just as much an expense as anything else you pay for in cash.

At this point I have good news for those of you who do only the "sales-in-the-mail" type of business. If you wish, you may legitimately skip section **a.** of this chapter and leap forward to the section called "Cash in the Mail." But to you retailers and sales-over-the-counter people, read on, because

35

it is important that you get a thorough grasp of cash across the counter.

a. CASH ACROSS THE COUNTER

All incoming cash (whether it be from across the counter or from anywhere else) comes from two separate and distinct sources. One source is REVENUE, and the other, for want of a better name, we must call NON-REVENUE.

Your revenue cash is easy to identify. It comes from payments for anything in the way of goods or services *that are paid for at the time of the sale*.

All other cash is non-revenue cash.

For instance,

> — money you put into the business
> — loans you receive
> — money collected by you and held in trust (e.g., employee deductions)
> — money collected by you from your charge customers is all non-revenue cash.

Do I hear a puzzled voice asking, "What's that last item? Don't charge collections come from sales?"

You're quite right, but stop and think a moment. If your charge sales are on an accrual basis and you collect a charge account, then you made the charge sale anywhere from a week or two months ago, and at that time you either listed it as a sale on your cash register tape, wrote out a sales slip, or put it down somewhere as part of the day's sales. You "recognized" it as part of the day's revenue, and since you've counted it once, you don't want to do it a second time.

In short, the whole business of revenue or non-revenue cash can be boiled down to three sentences:

(a) If all your sales are cash sales, then all your cash is revenue cash.

(b) If all your sales are cash sales *and charge sales on a cash basis*, then all your cash is revenue cash.

(c) If your sales are mixed cash and charge sales, *and your charge sales are on an accrual basis*, then you must know how much cash came from each source.

Now we are going to resort to subsections, but keep cool, because the whole business is very simple when taken step by step.

1. The daily cash sheet

(a) Cash sheet for cash basis sales

When your cash comes tinkling in you can do one of two things.

Method 1. You can list it either by ringing it up on your cash register, or writing it down somewhere to be added up later.

Method 2. You can put it in the cash drawer and forget about it.

The first method will give you a cash-received total at the end of the day; the second means you must count your cash to find out how much came in. The first method is best.

The second method will get by, but if you've been short-changed or somebody's tapped the till, you won't know it.

Method 1 calls for this kind of cash sheet:
You know that this much cash from sales came in

(cash register figure or slips added up)	$700.00
to which must be added the cash you had	
in the till at the start of the day	200.00
so that there should be a total on hand of	900.00
but, from this you paid out during the day	400.00
so you should have left	500.00
but after counting if up you find that you have only	484.00
which means that somebody short-changed	
you to the extent of	$16.00

That's the way most cash sheets go, although not necessarily with such unhappy results.

The purpose of the sheet is threefold: to provide in one place —

- — a sales total
- — a pay-out total
- — a cash shortage or overage figure

Method 2 calls for this kind of cash sheet

Cash on hand at the end of the day	$484.00
subtract cash in the till at the start of the day	200.00
	284.00
add the cash you would have had on hand if you hadn't paid it out for bills, etc.	400.00
which leaves the total which must have come in from sales during the day	$684.00

You will notice the $16 got lost in the shuffle, and that's the drawback of *Method 2*. It doesn't disclose the shortages or overages. Apart from that it is merely a rearrangement of the first cash sheet.

Now let's look at the actual details, as illustrated on the sample cash sheet in Sample #4.

Line 1: SALES. The total for the day, whether from the cash register, an adding machine tape, or from a column of figures on a piece of wrapping paper.

Line 2: OTHER INCOME. On this line goes all the money received by the business that is "not-sales." It may be revenue such as rent for space sublet, or it may be non-revenue, such as a loan for $200 from your uncle, or it may be the $100 weekend change fund you put into the till in the morning. You won't often have anything for this line, but when you do, be sure to put it in as otherwise your cash will be over at the day's end.

SAMPLE #4
DAILY CASH SHEET (No. 1)

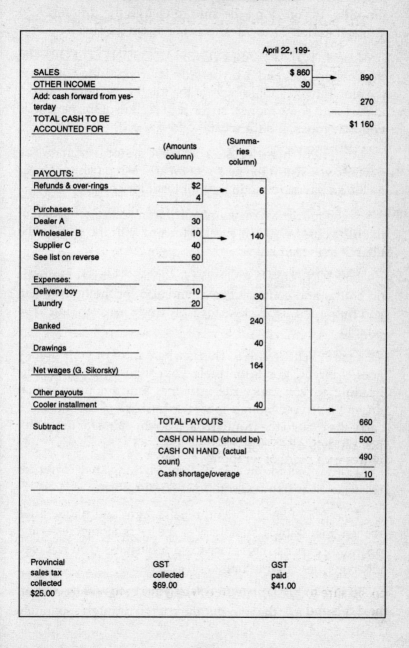

April 22, 199-

	(Amounts column)	(Summaries column)	
SALES		$ 860	890
OTHER INCOME		30	
Add: cash forward from yesterday			270
TOTAL CASH TO BE ACCOUNTED FOR			$1 160
PAYOUTS:			
Refunds & over-rings	$2	6	
	4		
Purchases:			
Dealer A	30		
Wholesaler B	10	140	
Supplier C	40		
See list on reverse	60		
Expenses:			
Delivery boy	10	30	
Laundry	20		
Banked		240	
Drawings		40	
Net wages (G. Sikorsky)		164	
Other payouts			
Cooler installment		40	
Subtract:			
TOTAL PAYOUTS			660
CASH ON HAND (should be)			500
CASH ON HAND (actual count)			490
Cash shortage/overage			10

Provincial sales tax collected $25.00	GST collected $69.00	GST paid $41.00

Line 3: CASH FORWARD FROM YESTERDAY. If you take the cash home at night, put back the same amount in the morning. If you don't, be sure to charge the difference to yourself under "Drawings," further down the sheet.

Line 4: TOTAL CASH TO BE ACCOUNTED FOR. The total of lines 1, 2, and 3. If you didn't pay anything out this is the amount you should have in the till. But, usually you had to part with some money, so the next section of the page tells you how much and for what.

And right here we stop to hoist a storm signal. The payouts you list in the next section are cash payouts. Never include a payment made by your business cheque.

A cheque drawn on your bank doesn't take money out of the till; your daily cash sheet is for use with the cash in the till, not in the bank.

Line 5: *REFUNDS AND OVER-RINGS*. This is for refunds on bottles and containers, etc., and also for the times when you ring up $1 by mistake for $0.10, (e.g., an over-ring of 90 cents).

Line 6: *PURCHASES*. This is where most of your money goes — buying goods for resale. Four sublines are under this heading so you can write in names and amounts. If that doesn't give you enough space use the back of the sheet and carry the total to the front. (In fact, do the same for any other pay-out when necessary.)

Do not include in this section anything that is not for resale, such as fixtures, equipment or furniture.

Line 7: *EXPENSES*. Rent, repairs, light and phone, fuel, scavenging, stamps, stationery — the list is a long one — any operating expense necessary to your business. You can read all about these in the chapter on expenses.

Line 8: *BANK DEPOSITS*. If your bank charges for collecting cheques, ask them to put the charge through separately and not to take it off the deposit, as is sometimes done. The total of the deposits on your cash sheet for the month should equal the deposits shown by the bank on your statement or passbook.

Line 9: *DRAWINGS*. This is cash taken out of the till for your personal use. It is not an expense, so don't call it wages. You can't pay yourself when you are working for yourself. What you can do is draw out some of the money you put into the business in the first place, or some of the profits you have made since.

Line 10: *NET WAGES*. If you have hired help and pay them by cash rather than by cheque, this is where you put their net take-home pay. This, of course, is not the total wage expense, but it is the total of the cash involved. You will find details on the wage deductions when you come to the chapter on payrolls.

If you hire casual help to clear snow from your sidewalks, put it in the expense section rather than under wages. In these days of innumerable payroll deductions, don't go out of your way to make work for yourself or your accountant.

Line 11: *OTHER PAY-OUTS*. A catchall for anything that doesn't fit anywhere else. For instance, here you can put —

> — down payments or installments on fixtures or other goods not for resale,
> — payments on a mortgage or on the purchase price of the business,
> — repayment of loans or money held in trust.

Items of this nature are better paid by cheque, so that you have a permanent record of the transaction. However, sometimes you may have more money in the till than in the bank.

Line 12: *TOTAL PAY-OUTS*. Add up all the pay-out summary figures in the middle column and shift the total, as the arrow indicates, to the right-hand column, so you can

41

subtract it from the "Cash to be accounted for" figure on line 4. The result, on

Line 13 is the cash you should have on hand. Count the cash in the till and put it on

Line 14 as cash by actual count. The difference between these two goes on

Line 15 and this is your shortage or overage for the day.

Cash shortages or overages are usually insignificant, but please note this: you can carry forward either the actual cash on hand or the theoretical, but whichever you do, be consistent. Don't do one way one day and the other way the next.

If you carry forward theoretical cash, then the difference on your cash sheet for the last day of the month will be your overage or shortage for the entire month.

If you carry forward actual cash, then your accountant will add up your overages and shortages separately and the net difference will be your overage or shortage for the month.

If you shortages and overages don't amount to a hill of beans, increase or decrease your daily gross sales figure so that the shortage or overage disappears. Bear in mind your time is worth more than penny detail.

(b) Cash sheet for cash sales plus charge sales on an accrual basis

Sheet No. 1A for this situation (Sample #5) is identical with its running mate, Sheet No. 1, *except* for the addition of lines to take care of charge account collections and charge sales. These two figures must be obtained by one of the methods outlined in the chapter on sales.

Lines 2A and 2B allow for this, so that you will still end up with cash to be accounted for on line 4.

There is one small problem you may encounter on this cash sheet, but there is an easy solution to it.

SAMPLE #5
DAILY CASH SHEET (No. 1A)

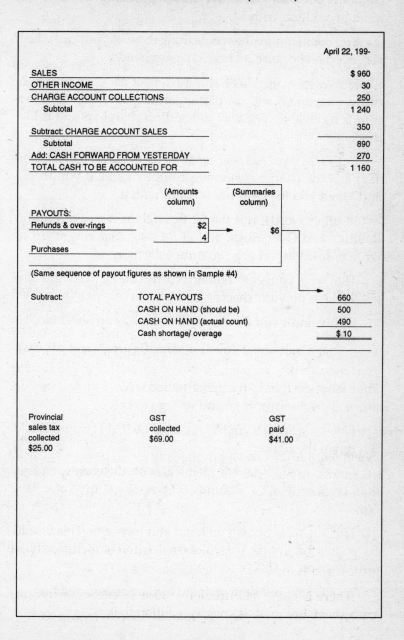

April 22, 199-

SALES	$ 960
OTHER INCOME	30
CHARGE ACCOUNT COLLECTIONS	250
Subtotal	1 240
Subtract: CHARGE ACCOUNT SALES	350
Subtotal	890
Add: CASH FORWARD FROM YESTERDAY	270
TOTAL CASH TO BE ACCOUNTED FOR	1 160

(Amounts column)   (Summaries column)

PAYOUTS:

Refunds & over-rings $2   → $6
4

Purchases

(Same sequence of payout figures as shown in Sample #4)

Subtract:		
	TOTAL PAYOUTS	660
	CASH ON HAND (should be)	500
	CASH ON HAND (actual count)	490
	Cash shortage/ overage	$ 10

Provincial sales tax collected $25.00	GST collected $69.00	GST paid $41.00

Suppose a charge customer walks in with an empty container, or some defective merchandise, and wants her account credited with $2.

You could ignore the whole thing so far as your cash sheet is concerned because no cash changes hands.

However, your sheet should reflect *all* your over-the-counter business and, in particular, any affecting your accounts receivable. The way to handle a charge refund is like this:

Enter it as if you had paid out $2 for the container (or merchandise) and the charge customer promptly handed you the $2 and asked you to credit her account with it.

In other words, put the $2 through as a pay-out under Refunds and Over-rings, and *at the same time* ring it up or write it down as a charge account collection.

That way, your cash remains correct and you should also get the facts on your sheet.

Below line 4 you do exactly the same as on Sheet No. 1.

(c) Cash sheet for "no-sales-figures" and all cash sales

The cash sheet (No. 2) for this situation is No. 1 turned upside down. Turn to Sample #6 and let's go over it:

Line 1: CASH ON HAND AT END OF DAY. Count it and put down the figure.

Lines 2 to 9: These are identical with the corresponding lines on Sheet No. 1 ("Refunds & Over-rings" to "Total Pay-outs.")

Line 10: Total of cash on hand and pay-outs. This would be your sales figure if you started from scratch, but you didn't, so, on.

Line 11 you put cash on hand at start of day, and on

Line 12 other income. The total of these two goes on

44

SAMPLE #6
DAILY CASH SHEET (No. 2)

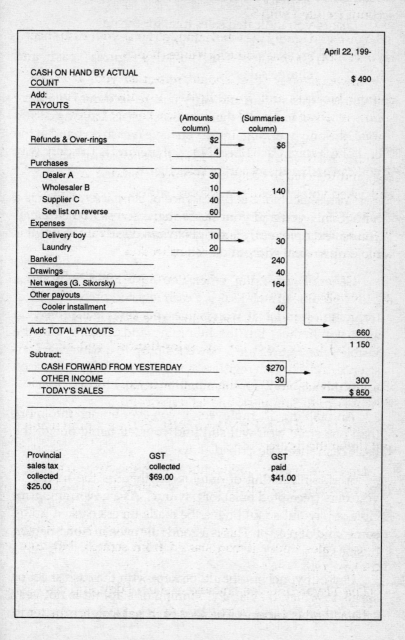

April 22, 199-

	(Amounts column)	(Summaries column)	
CASH ON HAND BY ACTUAL COUNT			$ 490
Add: PAYOUTS			
Refunds & Over-rings	$2		
	4	$6	
Purchases			
Dealer A	30		
Wholesaler B	10	140	
Supplier C	40		
See list on reverse	60		
Expenses			
Delivery boy	10		
Laundry	20	30	
Banked		240	
Drawings		40	
Net wages (G. Sikorsky)		164	
Other payouts			
Cooler installment		40	
Add: TOTAL PAYOUTS			660
			1 150
Subtract:			
CASH FORWARD FROM YESTERDAY		$270	
OTHER INCOME		30	300
TODAY'S SALES			$ 850

Provincial sales tax collected	GST collected	GST paid
$25.00	$69.00	$41.00

45

Line 13 where it can be subtracted from the figure on line 10, thereby giving you on

Line 14 you indicated sales total for the day.

(d) Cash sheet for "no-sales-figures" cash and charge sales

If you use this system and carry charge accounts, you have no option but to handle them on a cash basis. Lacking a sales total, the only working figure you have is cash on hand at the end of the day. Cash Sheet No. 2, therefore, is the only way you can arrive at any sort of sales figure.

Cash Sheet No. 2 is the essence of simplicity, which is a help if only you and your family have access to the cash. If you have employees, the simplicity is a disadvantage, as it is too easy to steal without detection.

Generally speaking, when you have hired help and a heavy volume of small sales, a cash register, preferably electronic, is essential. It won't give you complete protection against pilferage, but the humming and clicking and the visible sales figures are a powerful prop to a wavering conscience. Indeed, cash registers are sold as much for this reason as for the help they give in obtaining totals.

And talking of employees, if you ever branch into more than one store, you will still find yourself using one of the basic cash sheets described above.

And, still talking of employees, there is the matter of vouchers (receipted bills) for pay-outs. As a governing principle, a pay-out should never be made unless backed up by some kind of receipt. This is a good rule even in a one-person business.

Pay-out vouchers should be kept with the cash sheet or sheets to which they apply. Pinning or stapling is not very satisfactory as papers break loose and get lost. It is better to put, say, a week's vouchers in an envelope and staple the envelope to the sheet for the last day of the week.

If there are a great many vouchers each day (or where you have branch stores) a better plan is to use the envelope-type cash sheets. This is a regular sheet printed on the face of a large envelope. The vouchers go inside, the envelope is sealed, and nothing can get lost.

(e) To recapitulate

Now let us sit back and survey the ground you have covered with cash sheets — and that is not entirely a figure of speech. For, at the end of the month, you will have 21 to 31 cash sheets, depending on how many days a week you work. What use are these sheets, and why?

Well, we said before that the primary objects of a cash sheet are to provide a summary of the day's transactions and to find out if the cash is short or over.

At the end of the month, however, you are no longer thinking in terms of days, you want monthly figures. And the only way to get them is the hard way of adding all similar daily figures together.

Sounds like work, doesn't it?

So it is, but it's not as bad as it sounds.

The trick is to do a week at a time, so you never have more than seven daily figures to add, and if you've made a mistake, you don't have far to look.

Use a cash sheet monthly summary with the column headings you need. (See Samples #7, #8, #9, #10, #11, and #12.) On the summary sheet, each day has its line and each line must be arithmetically correct, just as your cash sheet is correct. Then, when you add up the week's figures, your week's totals will be correct.

Put the week's totals down and then go right ahead with the next week underneath. At the month end the results of

SAMPLE #7
CASH SHEET SUMMARY
(Cash basis sales)

Date	SALES	Other income	Cash forwarded	Total cash	Refunds & over-rings	Purchases	Expenses	Bank	Drawings	Net wages	Other payouts	Total payouts	Cash should be	Short	Over	Actual cash
1	860	30	270	1 160	6	140	30	240	40	164	40	660	500	10	—	490
2	800	—	490	1 290	10	110	20	500	—	—	—	640	650	—	10	660
3	760	—	660	1 420	4	60	40	800	—	—	—	904	516	6	—	510
4	700	—	510	1 210	8	80	20	600	—	—	—	708	502	—	8	510
5	890	—	510	1 400	10	40	50	850	100	—	—	1 050	350	10	—	340
6	764	—	340	1 104	2	8	40	600	—	—	—	650	454	4	—	450
7	—	—	—	—	—	—	—	—	—	—	—	—	—	—	—	—
Sub-total	4 774	30	—	—	40	438	200	3 590	140	164	40	4 612	—	30	18	—
8	800	30	450	1 280	6	54	20	700	40	164	—	984	296	—	4	300
9	820	—	300	1 120	—	36	50	600	—	—	50	736	384	4	—	380

and so on, for the full month, ending up with totals, like this:

	SALES	Other income	Cash forwarded	Total cash	Refunds & over-rings	Purchases	Expenses	Bank	Drawings	Net wages	Other payouts	Total payouts	Cash should be	Short	Over	Actual cash
	20 756	120		1 720	182		910	16 140	800	656	210	20 618		90	62	

SAMPLE #8
CASH SHEET SUMMARY
(Reverse side of Sample #7)

"EXPENSE" ANALYSIS

Delivery boy	$ 126
Advertising	116
Car expense	126
Repairs	98
Casual labor	60
Stamps & stationery	20
Fuel	124
Telephone	24
Laundry	140
Paper & supplies	76
	$910

"OTHER INCOME" ANALYSIS

Pay-phone commission	$ 50
Advertising space sublet	70
	$120

"OTHER PAYOUT" ANALYSIS

Cooler installment	$ 40
Spiff loan	170
	$210

CASH RECONCILIATION

Sales	$20 756
Other income	120
Cash forward from last day of last month	270
	21 146

PAYOUTS

Refunds & over-rings	182	
Purchases	1 720	
Expenses	910	
Banked	16 140	
Drawings	800	
Net wages	656	
Other payouts	210	20 618

Cash on hand should be	528
Net shortage/overage for the month	28
Actual cash on hand	$ 500

(forward to the first day of next month)

SAMPLE #9
CASH SHEET SUMMARY
(Cash and Accrual basis sales)

Date	SALES	Other Income	Charge A/c Collected	Sub-total	Charge A/c Sales	Sub-total	Cash forward	Sub-total	Refunds & Over-rings	Purchases	Expenses	Bank	Drawings	Net wages	Other payouts	Total payouts	Cash should be	Short	Over	Actual cash
1	960	30	250	1 240	350	890	270	1 160	6	140	30	240	40	164	40	660	500	10		490
2	840	—	280	1 120	320	800	490	1 290	10	110	20	500	—	—	—	640	650		10	660
3	750	—	260	1 010	250	760	660	1 420	4	60	40	800	—	—	—	904	516	6		510

This continues to the end of the month (with subtotals each weekend), ending up with totals as under:

| | 21 010 | 120 | 6 680 | | 6 934 | | | | 182 | 1 720 | 910 | 16 140 | 800 | 656 | 210 | 20 618 | 528 | 90 | 62 | 500 |

50

SAMPLE #10
CASH SHEET SUMMARY
(Reverse side of Sample #9)

"EXPENSE" ANALYSIS

Delivery boy	$ 126
Advertising	116
Car expense	126
Repairs	98
Casual labor	60
Stamps & stationery	20
Fuel	124
Telephone	24
Laundry	140
Paper & supplies	76
	$910

"OTHER INCOME" ANALYSIS

Pay-phone commission	$ 50
Advertising space sublet	70
	$120

"OTHER PAYOUT" ANALYSIS

Cooler installment	$ 40
Spiff Loan	170
	$210

CASH RECONCILIATION

Sales	$21 010
Other income (cash)	120
Charge A/c's collected	6 680
	27 810
Less: Charge A/c sales	6 934
	20 876
Add: Cash forward from last day of last month	270
Cash to be accounted for	21 146

PAYOUTS

Refunds & over-rings	182
Purchases	1 720
Expenses	910
Banked	16 140
Drawings	800
Net wages	656
Other payouts	210

20 618

Cash on hand should be	528
Net shortage/overage for the month	28
Actual cash on hand	$500

(forward to the first day of next month)

51

SAMPLE #11
CASH SHEET SUMMARY
(Cash basis — sales deduced)

Date	Actual cash on hand	Refunds	Purchases	Expenses	Banked	Drawings	Net wages	Other payouts	Sub-total	Cash forward	Other income	SALES
1	490	6	140	30	240	40	164	40	1 150	270	30	850
2	660	10	110	20	500	—	—	—	1 300	490	—	810
3	510	4	60	40	800	—	—	—	1 414	660	—	754
TOTALS	500	182	1 720	910	16 140	800	656	210	—	—	120	20 728

The payout figures on this summary are the same as those on Sample #7 and Sample #9.

The total sales figure is different because the proprietor had no way of knowing there was a net shortage of $28 during the month.

52

SAMPLE #12
CASH SHEET SUMMARY
(Reverse side of Sample #11)

"EXPENSE" ANALYSIS

Delivery boy	$126
Advertising	116
Car expense	126
Repairs	98
Casual labor	60
Stamps & stationery	20
Fuel	124
Telephone	24
Laundry	140
Paper & supplies	76
	$910

"OTHER INCOME" ANALYSIS

Pay-phone commission	$ 50
Advertising space sublet	70
	$120

"OTHER PAYOUTS" ANALYSIS

Cooler installment	$ 40
Spiff Loan	170
	$210

CASH RECONCILIATION

Cash on hand by actual count, last day of this month		$ 500
Add: PAYOUTS		
Refunds & over-rings		182
Purchases		1 720
Expenses		910
Banked		16 140
Drawings		800
Net wages		656
Other payouts		210
		$20 618
Less:		
Cash on hand last day of last month	$270	
Other Income	120	390
SALES for the month		$20 728

your work will be almost the equivalent of a cash sheet for the month, which is the usual period for writing up books.

It won't be exactly the equivalent of a cash sheet because there is still one small matter to be attended to before the job is complete.

The expense column in the summary is a *total* of expense pay-outs. If the tax department were satisfied with a total we could leave it at that, but they aren't — they want details. So the total of expense pay-outs must be broken down into the various kinds of expenses shown on your daily sheets.

You can put this breakdown on the back of the sheet where you have plenty of space. This same treatment should be given to any column total that covers diversified items. For instance, "other pay-outs" might consist of a payment on a mortgage, on a soft-drink cooler, and on a loan. It is not likely you will often have such an aggregation, but when you do, your accountant needs the details.

(f) Questions and answers

Before leaving the subject of daily cash sheets, let us deal with some minor perplexities that may bother you.

1. YOUR OWN CHEQUES COMING IN OVER THE COUNTER: Assume you have paid your employees by cheque, and one of them asks you to cash his or hers out of the till. Go right ahead, and treat the cheque as if it came from outside. Deposit it with any others you have on hand. *Don't, under any circumstances, tear it up.*

2. A CREDIT BALANCE IN CASH: This is your accountant's nightmare, so you had better know what it means, in case it ever comes up.

Briefly, it means your business is living without visible means of support. You have paid out more than you took in, and, so far as the records go, it is a case of pennies from heaven.

Of course, it isn't so. Money doesn't appear from nowhere any more than a government can live without taxes. The point is, somewhere along the line you forgot to put down that $400 loan from Uncle Albert, or the time your change fund was running low and you took $50 out of your pocket and put it in the till, or cash came in from some unusual source.

This couldn't happen, of course, if you kept a daily cash sheet. Yours cash would be over on that particular day and you would hunt down the overage.

But, presuming for the moment you weren't using a cash sheet, when your accountant ended up with a credit in cash at the month's end he would do one of two things:

> — He would ask you what happened, in which case you might remember about Uncle Albert.
> — He would not ask you about it and enter it in the books as sales you forgot to report, in which case it would be just fine for the tax department, but not so good for you.

The moral of this little squib is, "It pays to use a cash sheet."

3. RUBBER CHEQUES: A person may go through life without giving any rubber cheques (we'll concede a few do) but nobody can avoid getting them. If the bounce is temporary ("The bank made a mistake — put it through again, will you?") it won't entail any more than a redeposit, (by itself, and not with other cheques or currency) and your accountant, being intelligent, will notice the redeposit is the same amount as the charge-back and will offset one against the other.

But for the permanent or semi-permanent rubber cheque, the treatment is slightly different. You get it back from the bank, and the problem is, "Is it cash, or isn't it?"

If it is from a cash sale (or from a charge account when you are on a cash basis) tell your accountant that any NSF cheques not redeposited should be charged against sales. Then, if and when you do collect the cheque or part of it, you can ring it up as if it were another sale.

If it is from a charge customer and you carry your receivables on an accrual basis, tell your accountant to charge it to accounts receivable. Then, when the customer either redeems it or tells you to redeposit it, treat it as if it were an account collected and put it in the proper line on your cash sheet. If it never is made good, then at the end of the year, when you go over your accounts and weed out the duds, list it with any others and give the details to your accountant to write off as bad debts.

One more thing and then we can put aside the subject of cash sheets. For the sake of simplicity cash sheets are designed to record *only* the daily flow of cash in and out of a business, including taxes. It is essential to keep an accurate record of the amounts of provincial tax collected and, even more so, the amount of GST collected and paid out. Collection and remittance becomes routine, but the GST paid out represents recoverable money and merits your close attention. Also, it goes without saying that all underlying vouchers for both types of taxes should be kept for at least six years in case of future audits.

b. CASH IN THE MAIL

So far we have discussed only one type of business, where cash receipts are apt to be small individually, but continuous and substantial in the aggregate.

Now let's look at a different type of business, where sales and receipts are both larger and fewer, and therefore easier to handle.

You don't need a cash register for six or eight sales a day, nor a cash sheet, but you do need a cash book. It can be either a book by itself, or else part of an all-purpose book, such as a synoptic journal.

56

You will recall in the last chapter that the sales journal was a collection of sales figures arranged in columns so you could add them up easily and get the totals for the day, the week or the month, depending on what you needed. The cash book (or cash journal) works on exactly the same lines, with the column headings changed to fit the new situation.

Have a look at Sample #13. The first thing you'll notice is that several columns are exactly the same as those in the sales journal, but there are also some new ones, namely,

English	Accounting Equivalent
Miscellaneous pay-outs	Dr. General ledger
Miscellaneous income	Cr. General ledger

which are in the nature of catchall columns. And,

Goods purchased for resale	Dr. Purchases
Cash withdrawn for personal use	Dr. Drawings
Cash deposited in bank	Dr. Bank

all of which are self-explanatory.

Just as the two sets of columns, debit and credit, in the sales journal should add up to equal totals, so should the two sets of debits and credits in the cash journal. If they don't "cross-balance," check your arithmetic until the difference comes to light.

If you'd like to combine the sales journal and the cash journal into one book, there is no reason why you shouldn't provided you have enough columns. You can eliminate any duplicated column headings and save the space for any additional ones you think you may need.

One book or two books, the fundamentals are the same: the debits and credits of each entry must balance, and the debit and credit column totals on each page must balance. Keep this in mind and you can't go wrong.

And now let's take another step forward. We've dealt with incoming cash — what about outgoing cash?

SAMPLE #13
CASH BOOK

Date	Detail	General Ledger Dr.	General Ledger Cr.	Cash Dr.	Cash Cr.	Bank Dr.	Accounts receivable Cr.	Purchases Dr.	Discounts given Dr.	Sales Cr.	Drawings Dr.
2	Cash Sales			60						60	
	R. Spengle			83			83				
	B. Knight			37			37				
3	K. Weaver (2% discount)			147			150		3		
	Bank deposit				327	327					
4	P. Turner			220			220				
	Truck expense (towing)	30			30						
	Casual labor (R. Parks)	22			22						
	J. Spiff				50						50
5	Cash sales			168						168	
	Scrap metal (steel)				70			70			
	Tenant (shed sublet)		85	85							
	Wiping rags (supplies)	15			15						
	M. Pringle			375			375				
	Bank deposit				661	661					
	and so on, to the month-end.										
	JANUARY TOTALS	285	318	4,871	4,691	3,950	3,807	430	17	1,137	400

The principal outgo will be from your desk drawer or cash box to the receiving teller in the bank.

The columns in your cash book to take care of bank deposits are:

— Dr. Bank
— Cr. Cash

If you always bank all the cash that comes in, you can short-circuit the cash columns in your journal and jump directly from "Cr. Accounts Receivable" or "Cr. Sales" to "Dr. Bank." Thus, instead of making the entry:

Dr. Bank
   Cr. Cash

every time an account is paid, you wait until you make up your bank deposit and then put through a "compound" entry like this:

Dr. Bank	$500.00	
Cr. A/c Receivable (A B & Co)		$200.00
Cr. A/c Receivable (C D & Co)		250.00
Cr. A/c Receivable (E F & Co)		50.00

In accounting language, your are "recognizing" the incoming payment only when you deposit it.

It is a good rule to deposit all incoming cash. Customers' cheques go there anyway, and if anybody pays in currency, resist the temptation to slip a twenty into your wallet. If you don't, one day you will forget you extracted the twenty, the cash will be short, and there will be an uncomfortable atmosphere around the office.

However, if you're caught short one evening and really need the twenty, this is the entry that will take care of it:

Dr. Drawings	$20.00	
Cr. Cash		$20.00

If you only do it occasionally, you can put the "Dr. Drawings" in the "Dr. General Ledger" column. If you make a bad habit of it, you had best head up a column "Dr. Drawings" so you will have a month-end total without the work of picking it out from the catchall column.

c. PETTY CASH

"Petty Cash" is no more petty than other cash. The name comes from the French "petit," which means small, and it is small only by comparison with the money you have in the bank. If you are running a store or retail business and pay for small purchases with cash out of the till, for practical purposes you already have a petty cash fund, so don't bother with another.

If, however, nearly all your customers pay by cheque, and fairly large ones at that, then you will need something else to take care of the small cash purchases every business makes.

If you are by yourself, the simplest way is to pay for these things out of your own pocket, get a receipt and keep it in a safe place. Then, periodically you add up all the receipts and write yourself a cheque for the exact amount of the total.

This squares you, but it doesn't square the books, because the batch of small bills you have paid must be classified as different kinds of expenses, just like their big brothers.

Sort the bills in separate piles, add up each pile, and then on the face of an envelope write down something like this:
Cheque No. 201 — Petty Cash

Gas and oil	$17.50
Repairs	12.00
Stationery	9.63
Purchases	15.70
Light bill	19.56
	$74.39

(Includes GST $4.86)

Tuck the bills in the envelope, seal it up, and place it in the folder you give your accountant each month.

The next petty cash set-up is called an "imprest fund," meaning money that has been temporarily shanghaied out of a regular cash. Your start the fund by writing out a cheque to Petty Cash for $10, $25, $100, or whatever amount is required for approximately a week. This is cashed and the money put in the petty cash box or drawer, where it should be kept under the control of one person, *and one person only*.

Nothing breeds distrust quicker than joint access to the petty cash box. Give the keys to a clerk — she will have a tough enough time trying to remember whether *she* put back that quarter she borrowed. If everybody can borrow quarters, you will end up by losing an employee.

In the meantime we will suppose that your petty cashier has paid out the $74.39 listed above, and she has paid it out of the $100.00 put in to start the fund. She itemizes the expenses on an envelope as shown above, writes out a cheque for the $74.39, and presents it to you for signature. You sign, she cashes it, and puts the $74.39 back in the box. She places the envelope in the accountant's folder.

Simple, isn't it? There will be in the petty cash box at all times money and receipted bills equal to the original amount of the fund. That's the reason you replenish the box with the exact amount of the bills paid — so you will always have the same figure to balance against.

You can use the imprest fund principle for more things than petty cash. Suppose you have a salesperson who has to cover the countryside for a week at a time and you have to pay the travel expenses. Start a "Travel Imprest Fund" of $300.00 and give him or her the money (we'll presume you're dealing with trustworthy people). Then, at the end of each trip, when receipted bills and/or an expense account are turned in, you write another cheque for the exact amount to bring the fund up to par again. This can go on indefinitely until your employee finally takes off for Florida with $117.69 of the fund unaccounted for.

Having read this far, you may think that for a subject as simple as cash there seem to be an awful lot of complications. So there are, when you are merely reading about them.

You will find, though, that when it comes to actual practice, the complications disappear. Once you get a cash routine established, it becomes semi-automatic, like driving a car. It's a good thing, because if you had to figure out each step as you went along, you'd never get any other work done.

Keep in mind that the sole purpose of cash sheets and cash books is to chart the flow of money through your business.

If, as you go along, you find you can condense, modify or cut out any of the steps outlined in this chapter, as long as you don't lose needed detail, more power to you. There is nothing sacred about the layout of a cash record.

But even big business recognizes the need for a statement showing what happened to the shareholders' money. It is a part of the annual report called "Statement of Provision and Application of Funds," and is full of huge, mystifying subtotals.

For your part you don't have to impress any shareholders. You gather your daily cash sheets together, put the figures in sequence, and when you are through you have a short, lucid summary which says, in effect:

WHERE THE STUFF CAME FROM
AND
WHERE IT WENT

5
RECEIVABLES

a. RECORD-KEEPING

If you sell for cash only, you will have no bad debts, few returned goods, and a lot less bookkeeping. The chances are though, you will find that to get the most out of your business you have to give credit. When this happens you will be carrying charge accounts, or, to use the accounting term, "Accounts Receivable."

The simplest, oldest, and still the most common form of accounts receivable is a rack filled with counter books. This is the traditional corner-store or grocery system, and there is much to be said in its favor.

Each customer has his or her own book; charge account entries are made just as quickly as you can write down words and figures: you carry the balance forward from the bottom of one page to the top of the next, and you never have to add up more than one page at a time.

When your customer pays up, it goes in the book, and if there is an unpaid balance, it shows plainly with no chance of argument.

To find out the total of your accounts receivable at any time, you must add together all your customers' unpaid balances. This is an unavoidable task, no matter how small or large your business may be.

The next simplest way of keeping receivables takes a little more time but can result in a very neat set of books. It is called the "monthly statement-ledger" system, and is highly recommended by the manufacturers of business forms. (The fact that its operation necessitates the use of a large number of business forms is just a lovely coincidence.)

To start this system you will have to buy (from the business-form people) a small metal box, commonly called an autographic register, having a flat writing surface on its top. Before starting the box, you feed it raw materials in the form of a sheaf of continuous-fold invoices, leaving the top one in position to write on.

When in use, you write out the details of the sale on the topside invoice, turn the lever or handle, and lo, the box spews forth (or "ejects," as the salesperson says with greater delicacy) the original copy of the invoice. Inside itself the machine stows away in proper order various colored carbon copies where they won't get lost. At the same time a fresh invoice appears on top, all ready for the next sale.

It is the colored carbon copies that you are concerned with. At the end of the day you gather these up and enter the amounts in your customers' ledger, which deserves a few words on its own account, because it is a very different proposition from a rack of counter books.

Your customers' ledger consists essentially of a sheaf of month-end statements — you know the kind — three columns, one for charges, one for payments, and a third for the balance owing. (There's a picture of one in Sample #14.) They are in loose-leaf form, with holes punched in the left-hand margin so they can be kept in a binder in alphabetical order. You can pretty them up as much as you please with your firm's name, address, and sales propaganda, as long as you leave enough space for a couple of lines after "In account with" where you can write the customer's name and address.

This binder, loaded with blank statements, is your accounts receivable ledger for the month, one customer to a page (except for the very active accounts which spill over

Telephone: 555-1349

426 Naples St.
Roseville, Ont.
M8K 6Z2

JOSEPH SPIFF & CO.
General Machine Shop Work
"Trunnions our Specialty"

IN ACCOUNT WITH:

Excel Mfg. Co. Ltd.,
428 State Drive
Hamilton, Ont.
L8N 7H6

Jan. 19-   Terms: 30 days net

	Charges	Credits	Balance
Balance forward			17.96
Inv. No. 3429	24.00		
Inv. No. 3507	10.00		
Cheque received		17.96	
Inv. No. 3902	12.00		46.00

onto a second page). Behind each page, for reasons that will appear in a moment, is a piece of plain paper cut to exactly the same size as the statements and also punched to fit the binder. (All these things come from the business-form people who are old hands at the game.)

The first step at the beginning of the month is to go through your ledger and head up each page with a customer's name. Use a piece of carbon paper as you go along so that you can make a duplicate on the plain piece of paper behind each statement.

Nearly all your customers will have unpaid balances at the end of the month. when you head up the statements for the coming month, write "Balance Forward" on the first line of the statement proper, and fill in the amount in the left-hand, or charges column. If you forget to do this, some day a customer will forget that he or she owed a balance forward.

Once you have attended to these preliminary details you can go ahead with the more important business of writing up this month's entries.

Take the colored copies of the invoices each day from the box and enter the amounts in the charge columns of the statements to which they belong. One of your colored copies should then be filed in a box in alphabetical order (customers' names) and the other on a permanent file in numerical order. (Your invoices will all be pre-numbered consecutively.)

When you make the entry in your customer's account, you can fill in the date if you want to, although most people are content to do it only on the first line. It is a good idea, though, to jot down the serial number of the invoice in the space to the right of the date column.

So much for the charges. Now, what about when your customers pay up?

Certainly you will have to enter a customer's payments in the credit column of his or her statement. The question is: what's the most convenient way of keeping track of the payments as they come in?

There are three methods commonly in use. They are as follows:

Method 1: A register slip. You make out a receipt on a regular invoice, hand the original to the customer, and later credit his or her account from the carbon copy in the machine. This method has one very definite advantage: every transaction involving a charge account goes through the machine — no transaction, no slip. On the other hand you have to watch carefully not to confuse a receipt with a regular invoice, and thereby charge a customer with the money just paid in.

Of course, if you are putting cash sales through the box, you will have to separate the cash-sales slips from the charge-sales slips anyway, so you may figure you might as well put receipts through too.

Perhaps this sounds as if the whole process is confusing, but that isn't so. Each slip can be plainly marked to indicate whether the transaction is a cash sale, charge sale, or a collection on an account. You go by these when you sort your slips into three piles at the end of the day to get the three totals you need.

However, if you don't like adding up piles of slips you can switch to:

Method 2: If you have a cash register that —

(a) allows you to punch a symbol on the tape or, better, accumulates a separate total for charge collections, and

(b) has a tape sufficiently wide for writing in customers' names,

then you can use your cash register as a receipt record. You can enter credits to customers' accounts directly from information on the tape.

Of course, there is nothing to prevent you combining Methods 1 and 2. You can put cash sales, charge sales, and charge collections through the box and the cash register if you like.

Method 3: This requires a receipt book, preferably a three- or four-decker, so you'll have a lot of room. Make your entries in the statements from the carbon copies of the receipts.

Those are the three basic methods, and you can use one of them or all of them if it is any easier. The point to keep in mind is that somewhere you should have a legible, permanent record of who paid and how much he or she paid. Whichever method you decide on, try it out — but don't change from one method to another in midmonth.

b. MONTH-END TIME-SAVING

And now we come to the enchanting part of statement-ledger receivables. You may have noticed (it would be difficult not to, as the salesperson will have pointed it out five times) that all your ledger leaves have a line of perforations down the left-hand side. Thus, at the end of the month, all you do is tear out the ledger sheets, fold and mail them.

Whether or not you staple carbon copies of slips to the statements before you mail them depends on how trusting your customers are. In theory, the customer keeps the original slip at the time of the sale and later checks it off against your statement. In practice, the customer stuffs it into the glove compartment or some other equally unreliable place, and then when he or she gets your statement, wonders if it is padded. For this reason, if the box turns out enough copies it is a good idea to take the carbons from your customers' alphabetical files and attach them to the statements.

The last step is to remove all carbon copies of the statements from your binder, and after copying all the unpaid balances onto your new month's statements, file the old ones away in a bundle. You are then all ready to start the monthly receivables cycle again.

As might be expected, refinements of the above system have been developed and the most ingenious of these is a "write-it-all-at-one-time" device, otherwise knows as a peg-board.

It consists of a large flat, portable writing board, on which you carefully align on little pegs, with carbon paper between them, the following sheets:

- customer ledger page
- customer monthly statement
- sales journal

Thus, when you enter an invoice on the top sheet you automatically make the same entry on the other two. In theory, this does two things:

> — It eliminates errors in transcription, because you don't copy from a journal to a statement.
> — It saves time, because you write each entry once.

In practice, the time spent fiddling with the various papers to get them in and out of position is often equal to or more than the time you would spend making separate entries.

It does, however, produce a professional-looking customer's statement and the sales journal has a self-checking feature that limits errors in arithmetic. Further, if you wish, you can use the board for payroll cheques and other printed journals and ledgers (accounts payable, for instance) all of which the business-form people will be delighted to sell you.

c. THE TRADITIONAL LEDGER

We have discussed the simplest and the next simplest form of accounts receivable ledger and its variations. Now we come to the traditional form, used almost universally by medium-sized, non-retail businesses.

It is exactly the same as a statement-ledger, except —

(a) the sheets are permanent — you don't pull them out at the end of the month (if a customer wants a statement, you have to copy the details out of the ledger),

(b) because it is permanent you don't have to carry forward unpaid balances to a new sheet for the next month. You carry a running balance in the balance column, increasing it or decreasing it as invoices are issued or payments received.

In practice you need only figure out balances at the end of the month. It saves arithmetic, and the month-end is usually the only time you are interested in them.

Sometimes a minor complication will crop up, namely, a customer with a temporary credit balance. This happens when —

(a) you issue a credit note, and at the time your customer is paid up, or

(b) a customer makes a deposit against a future purchase, or

(c) a customer's account has been overpaid by mistake.

None of these things should cause any difficulty, provided you make sure these credit balances are not mistaken for debit balances. The best precaution is to resort at once to your red pencil (or red ink, if you have the stuff around) which, you will remember, means "the opposite of normal."

Either write the credit balance in red pencil, or else put *Cr.* in red alongside it, or use any other eye-catching symbol which will serve to set it apart from the others.

When you make up your month-end list of accounts receivable, (and you find it includes some credit balances) make *two* lists, one for the regulars and a second for the credit balances. Subtract the credit balances total from the debit balances total and you will have the correct *net* total of your ledger.

And that is about all that can be said on the subject of the receivables ledger. (We haven't finished with the accounts themselves yet.)

No matter how large your business may grow, even if you have a battery of accounting machines or computers, you will still adhere to the principles outlined here.

There is only one way to know how much a customer owes: put down the charge when she buys, credit her when she pays, and figure out the difference with simple arithmetic.

d. CONTROL OF CUSTOMER ACCOUNTS

How do you feel when a customer comes in and points out a mistake in addition or subtraction on his or her statement?

Probably the same as most of us — slightly sheepish, curious as to how it happened, and, for some reason, a bit peeved about the whole thing.

Question: Is it possible to have foolproof receivables, with practical certainty there are no mistakes in arithmetic?

Answer: Yes, if you use a control account.

Question: What is a control account?

Answer: The following definition of a control account is taken from an accounting textbook:

> Accounts Receivable-Control is the general ledger account controlling the subsidiary ledger of accounts receivable, and to which debit and credit totals from the books of original entry are posted. The balance in the control account should at all times agree with the sum total of the individual balances in the subsidiary ledger.

Suppose we tear this mass of verbiage apart on the chance that it conceals some brilliant thought.

To begin with, "control" is a misleading title. The control account doesn't control your receivables ledger any more than you control your mother-in-law, but, like that good lady, it tells you immediately if anything is wrong.

"Debit and credit totals from the books of original entry" can be translated freely as "total invoices and total collections for the month."

A "book of original entry" means any place where the above figures are added up or assembled. It might be a sales journal, an adding machine tape, or a piece of paper with a column of figures on it, so long as it gives you the total sales and collections for your charge business for the month.

71

And this is why your receivables control account should show the total of the money owed to you by your customers: If, at the start of the month, your

customers owe you	$1 000.00
and during the month you invoice them with	500.00
making a total of	1 500.00
and, during the month, you collect from them a total of	700.00
then, logically, the unpaid balances should add up to	$ 800.00

The example shows the fundamental idea behind all control accounts, and to minimize the risk of any misunderstanding, here is a simple illustration:

At the beginning of the month:

	Mr. A	Ms. B	Mr. C	This is the "Control Account"
	These are the individual accounts in your receivables ledger			
	$300.00	$400.00	$300.00	$1 000.00
Add the month's invoices	200.00	100.00	200.00	500.00
	500.00	500.00	500.00	1 500.00
Take off the month's payments	300.00	300.00	100.00	700.00
Leaving at the month-end balances of	200.00	200.00	400.00	800.00

To those of you who grasp figures in a twinkle, the above illustration is unnecessary. But there are a lot of non-twinklers in business, and frequently they can sell rings around the twinklers. So don't be impatient if we take one step at a time.

And besides, we will now use those figures to illustrate another point, so if you didn't read them, please go back and do so.

Suppose when you entered the collection in A's account you made a mistake in subtraction and showed him as still owing $300. Then, when you added up the unpaid individual

72

balances you would have a total of $900 against $800 in the control account, showing you that something was wrong.

e. HOW TO FIND AN ERROR

Differences between your receivables ledger total and the control account can come from only a few basic causes, and they are —

    (a) errors in adding or subtracting in individual accounts,

    (b) errors in your sales journal or cash book,

    (c) errors in copying figures.

Let us pause a moment and enlarge on (c). When you enter your invoices or receipts in your customers' individual accounts, as a general rule it is better to do it from the figure in your journal column than from the invoice or receipt itself, because then at least you will know that the figures in your receivables ledger are the same as the ones you add up to get your control account entries. You can, of course, still mistake a seven for a four, or an eight for a three, but the chances are 50% less than if you first wrote the amount of your invoice in the customer's account, and then wrote in your sales journal column.

But, to resume our list of errors —

    (d) making errors through entries in your customers' accounts without a corresponding figure in your journal columns.

This is the mistake most commonly made. Mr. A. strides into the store just before closing time and says, "Give me ten bucks worth of trunnions and stick it on my account."

"Sure thing, Mr. A," you reply, and you enter the figure in his account then and there so you won't forget it.

And then and there you strip a gear in your control mechanism. For if the sale isn't in your sales journal column, then the column total for the month will be short of what it should be, and your control account balance at the end of the month will be short by the same amount.

And remember, the same thing can happen with credits.

One final thing about control accounts.

If you keep your own receivables ledger and make all the entries in it, then it is up to you to run down your own differences if you are out of balance. It is not cricket to make somebody else do it.

Nothing induces a feeling of frustration so much as hunting for somebody else's error, and your accountant, being only human, is apt to relieve his feelings with a good stiff fee.

f. SPECIAL RECEIVABLES

We could put it in the form of a riddle: "When is a receivable not a receivable?" and the answer, "When it is in hock."

Certain types of businesses, such as household appliance and furniture stores and car dealers, would be hard put to cover their overhead, let alone make a profit, if they had to depend entirely on cash sales. Therefore, they resort to one or more methods of financing sales over periods from three months to three years.

These are:

Method 1: The dealer does his or her own financing. This is usually only for small amounts and short periods. The average dealer hasn't the capital for more, nor the time for the necessary bookkeeping.

Method 2: The dealer *appears* to do his or her own financing. Actually, the accounts are turned over to a finance company when the deal is completed, with the dealer receiving at that time anywhere from 60% to 100% of the amount the customer owes.

The amount of the "holdback" is put to the dealer's credit in a "reserve" account on the finance company's books, against which the finance company can charge back any uncollectible accounts. Sometimes the finance fee is paid by the customer and sometimes the dealer absorbs it as an expense of doing business.

This type of financing requires careful attention to customers' installment payments. Frequently the finance company furnishes a coupon book to facilitate identification of the account. The dealer is expected to remit these payments promptly and regularly with a list (or the coupons themselves) showing who paid and how much. They are, in a sense, funds received in trust, in that they belong to the finance company and not to the dealer, and they should be kept preferably in a separate bank account.

If you are using a daily cash sheet, this type of receipt goes under "other income," and it is important that you explain the set-up fully to your accountant so he can match receipts from customers with payments to the finance company.

The theory behind this method is that it keeps customers coming into the store, where they can be inveigled into buying something else. Sometimes it has the opposite effect, the customers thinking as they walk in the door, "Well, here we go again. 'Easy payments,' my foot!"

Method 3: The dealer signs up the customer on a contract provided by the finance company and the customer makes payments directly to the finance company thereafter. The dealer then has no further concern with the account, *unless* the customer falls down on the payments and the goods are repossessed. The balance owing is then charged to the dealer, either against his "holdback" fund, or else as a current bill requiring prompt payment.

The holdback money retained by the finance company eventually is turned over to the dealer (less any sour accounts that have been charged against it). Whether this fund is paid bit by bit as each account is cleared, whether it is paid in chunks at various times, or whether payment is deferred until some indefinite future date, depends on the arrangement made. Naturally the finance company will prefer the last named set-up, as it enables them to snowball the holdback account to a size where eventually they are protected against any conceivable repossession loss.

There is another point to keep in mind when agreeing to a holdback scheme. Most finance companies are reputable houses. They maintain adequate records, live up to their promises and conduct business on strictly ethical lines. There are, however, finance companies that are not averse to pocketing such portions of the holdback fund as they can get away with. This, of course, is possible only if the dealer has no reliable record of what goes into and what is charged against the fund, which is a powerful argument for keeping proper records if you go in for installment sales.

Method 4: Another type of pledged receivable is represented by an account on which you have drawn a draft or trade acceptance and which you have discounted (either before or after acceptance) with your bank. There is nothing difficult about recording this. You credit your customer's account when the draft has been accepted and the bank has discounted it and put the proceeds in your account.

Dishonored drafts should be charged back against the customer immediately when the bank advises they have been returned unpaid.

Method 5: If you are loaded with cash, you can sell goods on the installment plan without going near a finance company. This calls for nothing more than a regular accounts receivable ledger and a sales and cash journal for control purposes (don't try to carry installment receivables without a control account — they can get out of hand in no time).

Certainly you are entitled to a finance fee for your services, and this revenue should be given a special column in your sales journal so you can tell if you are getting enough to compensate for the extra trouble.

Be careful, though, that you don't get out of your depth, because running a finance company is a specialized business in itself. Proceed very slowly and consult your accountant every step of the way.

6

PAYABLES

It is the exceptional thing to carry on a business without owing money, and for this you should be thankful. For, unless you are so wealthy that you can pay spot cash for everything, you will be using other people's money (in the form of "accounts payable") continuously to help stretch out your own. Of course, if you in turn sell on credit terms, then you are helping out other people with your money, and so the wheels go around.

Accounts payable is the accountant's way of saying "the money you owe." Nearly always it is used in the sense that the debt is for stock-in-trade or ordinary running expenses, commonly known as Trade Accounts payable.

True, all the money you owe is payable to somebody at some time, but the non-trade payables such as withholding tax, sales tax, mortgages, agreements to purchase and the like, are usually shown separately in any list of creditors. This is because they are either preferred or secured debts, and in the event of your business folding up, they will be paid first, while the rest of your creditors scrabble for what's left.

a. KEEPING PAYABLES ON A CASH BASIS

Just as with accounts receivable, there are two ways of handling accounts payable, and that doesn't mean paying them or not paying them. There is a cash basis (when paid) and the accrual basis (when made). And also, just as with accounts receivable, the cash basis is by far the simpler of the two.

The cash basis means that your accountant enters in your books various purchases you make and expenses you incur *when* he comes across the cancelled cheques or receipt that shows payment has been made.

He worries neither himself nor you about the bills you have run up, whether you pay them when due or past due, in full or in part. That he leaves to you, just as he leaves the job of checking prices, extensions, and additions on your suppliers' invoices.

The only time he concerns himself with unpaid bills is when he is about to take off an income statement, because then he must be sure that the full cost of all the goods you have sold and all your operating expenses appear on the statement. If he didn't include unpaid bills, then your purchases and operating expenses would be short by those amounts.

There are three reasons why keeping accounts payable on a cash basis in a small business is simple and satisfactory.

First, there are relatively few accounts, often not more than 10 or 15, frequently less.

Second, most of your suppliers will send you monthly statements showing invoices and payments, both of which can be checked off easily.

Third, you may occasionally forget to pay a bill, but it is a rare thing when your creditor forgets too.

That the cash basis of keeping payables yields exactly the same figure for expenses as the accrual basis may be readily seen if you compare the two side by side:

CASH BASIS (When Paid)

Actual cash paid or cheques given to suppliers during the month	$1 800.00
Add: Unpaid purchase invoices at the end of the month	1 680.00
	$3 480.00

Subtract: Unpaid purchase invoices at the	
start of the month	1 460.00

Actual purchases figures for month	<u>$2 020.00</u>

ACCRUAL BASIS (When Made)

Actual purchases for the month, whether paid	
or unpaid, according to a "purchase journal"	
or other means of listing purchases	<u>$2 020.00</u>

In the illustration above we used "purchases." The same procedure is applied to all your other expenses, such as supplies, advertising, light and power, and the rest. That's why, when your accountant asks you for a list of your accounts payable at the end of the year, he does not want a lump total. He wants it broken down into so much for purchases (always the largest figure), so much for supplies, and so on.

The cash basis of payables accounting is absolutely accurate. It is used by public accountants for the majority of small businesses, though like cash-basis receivables, you will rarely find any mention of it in bookkeeping texts.

b. KEEPING PAYABLES ON AN ACCRUAL BASIS

The accrual basis takes a little more time, although not so much as accounts receivable, because, again, there are fewer accounts and therefore fewer entries.

If you decide to keep accrual payables, you will need a payables control account because without it you might as well stick to a cash basis and rely on your creditors' monthly statements for information.

Control means "Columnizing" your monthly bills, and so you will need a journal. Call it an expense journal, purchase journal or whatever you please, its function is parallel to that of the sales journal, namely, to collect and summarize information for the month so you have proper totals to work with (see Sample #15).

As with the sales journal, you have two sets of columns, debit and credit, and, on any page the dollar totals of the two sets must be equal (cross-balanced).

You don't need many column headings. The most important is "Cr. A/c Payable," and in it goes the amount of every bill you incur. Its running mate will be "Dr. Purchases" mostly, but every so often it will be "Dr. Paper & Wrapping Supplies, or Dr. Laundry Service, Dr. Car Expense," or some other frequently incurred expense. You will also need a "General Ledger" catchall column for those bills that come only once or twice a month, and hence do not need a column to themselves.

When you are buying from a supplier all through the month, it's not necessary to journalize every one of the invoices as they come in. Keep them in a folder until the month-end statement arrives. Check off the invoices against the statement and enter only the statement total in your journal. If the supplier is willing to save you a lot of detail work, let him or her do so.

In addition to the regular columns you will have an important new column, the one for the GST. The tax will have been applied by your creditors to every purchase you make and every expense you incur and it represents refundable money. The column total will likely be your largest input tax credit, so treat it with respect.

In the course of the month, then, you will have written up your journal so that the Cr. Accounts Payable column will give you the total of all the bills you have incurred during the month, and the various debit column totals will show you the expense classifications into which they fall, including GST and a mixed lot in the Dr. General Ledger column.

Once more we turn to accounts receivable for a comparison. You will remember that sometimes a customer returned goods, and to handle the entry you had the choice of putting

SAMPLE #15
PURCHASE JOURNAL

Date	Detail	General ledger Dr.	General ledger Cr.	Purchases Dr.	GST Dr.	Frght in Dr.	cartage out Dr.	Truck expense Dr.	Accounts Payable Dr.	Accounts Payable Cr.	Cash Dr.	Cash Cr.
2	National Metals Inc.			174	12					186		
3	Weller Tool Supply			89	6					95		
3	Acme Scrap Metal			40	3							43
4	Reliable Transfer				2	32				34		
4	Ace Fuels Inc. (Oil)	92			7					99		
	Newman Garage				4			55		59		
5	National Metals (goods returned)			(27)	(2)				29			
	Western Power (light and power)	129			9					138		
6	P.Q. Cartage				1		12					13
	Sure-Weld Inc.			280	20					300		
	JANUARY TOTALS	596		3 075	256	177	98	183	54	4 249		190

82

NOTES ON SAMPLE #15

And so on, to the end of the month. In fact, for most of your entries in this journal you will have to wait until after the end of the month because your suppliers' statements won't be in until then. (The above entries are from firms that don't send statements).

The entry in brackets in the Purchases column is a credit. It could have been entered in the Cr. General ledger column, but keeping it in the Purchases column makes one less entry at the month end. It will be subtracted from the total of the other Purchases column figures when you add the column.

red figures in the Cr. Sales column and Dr. A/c Receivable column, or alternatively heading up "Dr. Returns and Re-funds" and "Cr. A/c Rec."

So with payables. When *you* return goods, you can either put red figures (or "ringed" figures) in the Dr. purchases and Cr. A/c payable columns, or alternatively, head up columns Dr. A/c Payable and Cr. Returned Goods, whichever is more convenient.

Most of your payables will be paid by cheque and for this you use the Dr. Accounts Payable and Cr. Bank columns. For the occasional account paid by cash, use the Cr. Cash column. Cash and Bank columns can be written in whichever journal you wish, but they are usually located in your cash journal. It is handy to have all cash entries in one journal, rather than several, although there is no fixed rule about it.

For your accounts payable control account, the totals you need are at the bottom of the Dr. and Cr. A/c Payable columns.

To illustrate the procedure for payables control, let us suppose that at the start of the month there are individual accounts in your accounts payable ledger as shown on page 87.

Your accounts payable ledger is no different from a re-ceivables ledger, except that the name at the top of each page is that of a creditor and the balances are credit balances.

Sometimes there may be a temporary debit balance in a creditor's account. When this happens at the month-end, add up these debit balances separately and subtract this separate total from the total of your regular credit balances. Only by doing this will you balance with your control account figure.

CONTRA-ACCOUNTS: If you sell Joe Spiff groceries and Joe sells you fuel oil, the question will arise, "Why not offset my account against Joe's account and save mailing cheques?"

I once heard an accounting machine salesperson suggest that those who contra-accounted should have their right arms cut off at the elbow. That, of course, is silly (two fingers would be sufficient) but, nevertheless, don't contra-account if you can avoid it. It is a frequent cause of errors, makes for extra accounting work, and often leads to bad feelings.

However, there will be occasions when contra-accounting is forced on you. Joe owes you $75 and you owe Joe $100, and Joe is too hard up to let you have a cheque for $75. It's your year-end and you want to clear off old accounts, so you send Joe a cheque for $25.

The journal entry for the cheque is simple enough:

Dr. Accounts payable (Joe) $25.00

Cr. Bank $25.00

That leaves $75 sitting in Joe's account payable and the same amount in Joe's account receivable. To clear these balances, the entry is:

Dr. Accounts payable (Joe) $75.00

Cr. Accounts Receivable (Joe) $75.00

If you use your payables journal for this entry, you will have to put the credit in the Cr. General Ledger column, because it's not likely you have a special column for Cr. Accounts Receivable. If you use the sales journal, the same situation exists, in that you'll have to put the debit in the Dr. General Ledger column.

Alternatively, you might start up a special two-column book called the General Journal, into which you can put all entries that don't seem to fit anywhere else.

Or better still, wait until you've read chapter 7 and know how to set up a synoptic journal.

But, whatever you do, make the entries to your receivables and payables ledgers from a journal, and not directly in the accounts.

When you post a creditor's invoices (or monthly statement total) it is safer to do it from the payables journal, rather than from the invoice or statement itself, as this cuts out a possible error through miscopying, or even forgetting to enter the figure in the journal.

As to the kind of ledger you use for your accounts payable, you can suit yourself. Bear in mind that the pages must have three columns — debit, credit, and balance — and there should be enough pages to give one to each supplier you normally deal with. For your occasional creditors you can head up "A Sundry," "B Sundry," etc., pages and save space.

Whether the pages are ledger leaves, a tray of cards, or a schoolroom scribbler does not matter as long as you have enough writing space and keep it orderly.

But, remember, if you set up an accounts payable ledger and make the entries therein yourself, then it is up to you to see your ledger is in balance with your control account.

	Owed to D. & Co. $400	Owed to F. & Co. $500	Owed to G. & Co. $600	Payables Control A/c $1 500
During the month you buy goods from each amounting to..............	$200	$300	$400 (Cr.A/c Payable column total)	$900
so that you then owe them..............	$600	$800	$1,000	$2 400
but during the month you pay them..............	$400	$500	$300 (Dr.A/c Payable column total)	$1 200
so that at the end of the month you owe them..............	$200	$300	$700	$1 200

7

THE SYNOPTIC JOURNAL

By the time you get to this chapter, unless you have skimmed and skipped, you should have a fair understanding of the mechanics of bookkeeping.

Before going further it will be a sound idea to bolster that understanding with some theory. Rule-of-thumb is fine up to a point, but when you run up against something not covered by the rules, you need "know-why" as well as "know-how."

Therefore, let us have a look at the fundamental idea underlying the whole complicated structure of bookkeeping and accountancy. You will find that, like most fundamentals, it is simple. Here it is:

There are two sides to every transaction — somebody gives something and somebody gets something.

Put into accounting language, this means the party who *gets is debited,* and the party who *gives is credited.*

When I say "party" it is for the sake of ease in remembering, because obviously it is not always a party that gives or gets. It may help, though, to think of the accounts as persons if you have trouble figuring out which is the debit and which is the credit. Thus, a common transaction (when you make a charge sale) is:

(Accounting entry)	*("Personalized" as:)*
Dr. A/c Receivable $10.00	A/c Receivable gets $10.00 worth of goods
Cr. Sales　　　　 $10.00	Sales gives $10.00 in revenue

and another common one (when you issue a cheque for merchandise) is:

Dr. purchases $50.00   Purchases gets $50.00 worth
                                                      of goods

Cr. Bank $50.00   Bank gives out $50.00

Now, you may ask, "What is the point of showing the two sides of every transaction? Whey not just put down 'Sales — $10' or 'Purchases — $50' and let it go at that?"

You can if you want to. In fact, if you put down all your revenue and expenses with meticulous care and sum them up absolutely accurately at the end of the year, you will know exactly how much profit you made. A lot of small businesses do just that. It is known as single-entry bookkeeping.

The catch is that if you make a mistake in addition or subtraction, or in copying a figure from one page to another, you'll never know it. You may feel you made more or less money than the figures showed, but you've had it drilled into you that "figures don't lie."

But they can and do — if you rely on single-entry bookkeeping. This is why double-entry is so popular — it reduces the chances of errors in arithmetic to near zero. It still won't show a mistake of $10 too much in the credits if you've also made a mistake of $10 too much in the debits, but a double error like that happens very rarely. So rarely that if your double-entry books are in balance you can stop worrying and sleep soundly.

And now, having sold you, I hope, on the benefits of double-entry bookkeeping (your accountant will set up your books on a double-entry basis whether you are sold or not) let me say that every transaction in your business, from the sale of penny candies to a chrome-plated pleasure cruiser, resolves itself into a debit and credit entry, and that the sole purpose of cash sheets and journals is to collect and summarize these deals so you won't get bogged down in a statistical swamp.

Just as a daily cash sheet may represent 200 sales, so a cash sheet summary or a sales journal page may represent 20 or 30 daily totals, and so, again, your year's income statement will represent 12 monthly totals. The whole scheme of book-keeping is devoted to collecting and summarizing figures into final totals.

You have read about collecting figures in three or four places — the cash sheet, sales journal, cash journal and payables journal. What about sliding all these together so you have just one journal instead of several?

Absolutely yes — as long as the pages are wide enough to give you all the columns you need. In fact, most small businesses get by with one journal. It is called a "synoptic," which is a word of Greek origin meaning, roughly, "see everything at once."

You probably noticed that the Cash columns are present in each journal, as are also the catchall General Ledger columns. In a synoptic, once is enough. Ordinarily you work you way down the page, one line at a time, so it stands to reason you will only have one entry at a time in your Cash, General Ledger, or any other frequently used column.

A synoptic journal for a small business will always have the following columns:

Dr. Bank
Cr. Bank
Dr. General ledger
Cr. General ledger
Dr. Cash
Cr. Cash
Dr. Purchases
Cr. Sales
Dr. Drawings

and frequently:

Dr. A/c Receivable
Cr. A/c Receivable
Dr. A/c Payable
Cr. A/c Payable
Dr. Wages
Cr. Employee tax deductions
Cr. Canada Pension Plan
Cr. Unemployment Insurance

Other columns depend on whether you have other items which occur sufficiently often during the month to warrant a column.

Expenses such as telephone, light and power, rent, fuel, etc., rarely occur more than once a month, and hence the debit side of these entries can be placed in the Dr. General Ledger column, to be sorted out later.

In fact, you can adopt as your motto, "When in doubt put it in the General Ledger column." That way you can always cross-balance your page when you reach the bottom line. Every entry in the General Ledger column has to be dealt with separately, so there is no danger of anything being overlooked.

Now let's check off the sources your business figures come from and see how they fit into the synoptic journal columns.

a. CASH SHEETS

Suppose you are on a strictly cash basis and the cash sheet totals for the month are those at the foot of the summary columns in Sample #7. Have a look at Sample #16 and you will see how those same figures are spread across the synoptic journal.

You will be struck with the similarity between the two layouts, which is not surprising. For so far as cash transactions

SAMPLE #16
SYNOPTIC JOURNAL
(Tie-in Sample #7)

Date	Detail	Check #	General Ledger Dr.	General Ledger Cr.	Bank Dr	Bank Cr.	Cash Dr.	Cash Cr.	Purchases Dr.	Sales Cr.	Drawings Dr
30	Cash analysis				16 140		20 876	20 618	1 720	20 756	800
	Pay phone commission			50							
	Advt. space sublet			70							
	Refunds		182								
	Net wages due		656								
	Cooler payment		40								
	Spiff loan		170								
	Cash shortage		28					28			
	Delivery boy		126								
	Advertising		116								
	Car expense		126								
	Repairs		98								
	Casual help		60								
	Stamps & stationery		20								
	Fuel		124								
	Telephone		24								
	Laundry		140								
	Paper & supplies		76								

If you total the columns to this point they will cross-balance. True, the layout is somewhat lopsided, but there is no alternative because each expense must be itemized. The lopsidedness is less when the checks are written in, like this.

Date	Detail	Check #	General Ledger Dr.	General Ledger Cr.	Bank Dr	Bank Cr.	Cash Dr.	Cash Cr.	Purchases Dr.	Sales Cr.	Drawings Dr
2	Whalen & Company	72				275			275		
	J. Spiff	73				125					125
	Newman Garage										
	(truck expense)	74	152			152					
		75	500			500					
	Nelson Metals Inc.	76				482			482		

and so on, to the month end. If every month were like this you could reduce the width of the page by putting the Dr. Bank, Dr. Cash, Cr. Cash and Cr. Sales in the Dr. and Cr. General Ledger columns. Sometimes an accountant will break with tradition and actually do this.

Date	Detail	Check #	General Ledger Dr.	General Ledger Cr.	Bank Dr	Bank Cr.	Cash Dr.	Cash Cr.	Purchases Dr.	Sales Cr.	Drawings Dr
	JANUARY TOTALS		4 207	1 080	16 140	14 572	20 876	20 646	14 306	20 756	1 525

go, the synoptic is merely the cash sheet summary with makeup on. The bone structure is identical.

Before entering any of these figures in the synoptic, it is a good idea to add up the debits and credits separately on a piece of paper; then you can be sure the totals are equal and the cash entry will therefore cross-balance.

Note that nowhere in the journal will you find your cash on hand at the start or finish of the month. This is because the journal is concerned only with what happened during the month, and not what happened before or afterwards. The before and afterwards is in a book called the general ledger, and that is another part of the forest which we will explore shortly.

To return to cash sheets, if you run your receivables on an accrual basis you will have two additional entries to put in your synoptic journal. Suppose the totals for the month are those at the foot of the summary columns in Sample #9. Look at Sample #17 and you will see how receivables are handled in the synoptic.

The rest of the cash sheet summary items follow in order, with pay-outs charged in the appropriate debit columns, and a credit in Cash column for the total paid out.

Again, no attention is given to cash on hand at the start or finish of the month.

b. RECEIVABLES AND PAYABLES

Enough has been written about these and their journals in their own chapters, so we won't say more here.

Whether the entries arise from "across-the-counter" transactions or "in-the-mail," your synoptic journal columns will take care of debits and credits as illustrated in Samples #17 and #18.

The bookkeeper who wrote up the synoptic in Sample #18 was just starting to keep books and put every entry in,

Date	Detail	General Ledger Dr.	General Ledger Cr.	Bank Dr.	Bank Cr.	Cash Dr.	Cash Cr.	Accounts Receivables Dr.	Accounts Receivables Cr.	Purch. Dr.	Sales Cr.	Draw. Dr.
	Cash Analysis			16140		20876	20618	6934	6680	1720	21010	800
	Pay phone commission		50									
	Advt. space sublet		70									
	Refunds	182										
	Net wages due	656										
	Cooler payment	40										
	Spiff loan	170										
	Delivery boy	126										
	Advertising	116										
	Car expense	126										
	Repairs & maintenance	98										
	Casual help	60										
	Stamps & stationery	20										
	Fuel	124										
	Telephone	24										
	Laundry	140										
	Paper & supplies	76										
	Cash shortage	28					28					
	Wages (G.S.)	144										
	(Cr. tax withheld)		112									
	(Cr. C.P.P.)		12									
	(Cr. U.I.C.)		20									
	Whalen & Company				275					275		
	J. Spiff				125							125
	Newman Garage	152			152							
	(truck expense)											
	W. Blandford (rent)	500			500							
	Bank loan (4 mo. note)		1000	960								
	Bank discount charged	40										
	January Totals	6307	2764	18155	17962	20876	20646	6934	6680	15290	21010	1500

The $28 credit in the Cash column is there to remind you that although it is not included in your list of payouts, cash shortage is a cash expense just like the others, and Cash must be credited accordingly.

Your accountant would probably put $20 646 at the head of the Cash credit column and omit the $28 entry. Cash overages, of course, mean a corresponding debit in the Cash debit column.

and so on, to the end of the month. The proprietor of this business doesn't keep a payroll book, so he shows the $144 withheld from his employee as a debit to "wages" in the general ledger debit column, with the balancing credits for income tax, C.P.P., and U.I.C. as shown above. Thus the correct total of $800 wages gets entered in the books.

SAMPLE #18
SYNOPTIC JOURNAL

Date	Ck. No.	Detail	Inv. No.	General Ledger Dr.	General Ledger Cr.	Bank Dr.	Bank Cr.	Cash Dr.	Cash Cr.	Wages Dr.	Income Tax Cr.	U.I.C. Cr.	C.P.P. Cr.	Purch. Dr.	Sales Cr.	Accounts Receivable Dr.	Accounts Receivable Cr.	Accounts Payable Dr.	Accounts Payable Cr.
	371	J. Shields					361			480	102	9	8						
	2	H. Burke					280			360	66	8	6						
	3	J. Williams					505			672	149	9	9						
	4	K. Pudleigh					199			240	32	5	4						
	5	F. Knight					293			400	76	9	6		16				
		H. Weaver	891												190	190			
		B. Little	892												254	254			
		D. Frances	893												319	319			
	376	Wheeler & Company					487											487	
	7	Sign-Ad Company					56											56	
	8	H. Blandford (rent)		500			500												
		P. Buckie						415									415		
	9	Hoover Co. (bldg. repairs)		64															64
		Reliable Motors Inc.					96											96	
		Wheeler & Company												268					268
		Bank Loan		200			200												
		D. Frances						319									319		
		Bank deposit				734			734										
	380	Petty Cash		75			75												
		Reliable Motors Inc. (car exp.)		112															112
		and so on, to the end of the month.																	
				2437		12670	13474	12670	12670	8874	1496	163	131	3756	13481	13481	12670	4117	3920

95

one line at a time, to be absolutely sure each line cross-balanced.

Sample #19 is the way the same page would be written up six months later. The bookkeeper has caught on to all sorts of shortcuts and time savers, which are discussed below:

Comments on Sample #19

1. Pay-cheques: he now puts through the totals from the payroll book, instead of writing out each individual cheque. He might go further than this and leave out the payroll cheques entirely, posting from the payroll book to the general ledger. His boss, however, likes everything to go through the synoptic, so he puts them in.

2. Accounts receivable debits: instead of writing out a corresponding credit to sales for each invoice, he waits until he has a week's or a month's invoices entered, then adds them up and puts the total in the Cr. Sales column.

3. Accounts receivable credits: he follows the same procedure here and, in fact, goes further. He cuts out the cash columns by not "recognizing" payments from customers until he deposits them in the bank.

With both debits and credits to accounts receivable he saves space and writing by putting both on the same line when they are for the same customer.

4. Accounts payable: he also adopts the same-line procedure for debits and credits here.

The net result of these short cuts is a saving of 6-figure columns, 21 lines, and 34 entries. Two extra columns are required for "names" but the overall saving is well worthwhile.

This is about as many columns as you can comfortably handle in one book (you can get them up to 36 columns wide). As the business grows it would be better to extract the Sales and Receivables columns and place them in a separate Sales

SAMPLE #19
SYNOPTIC JOURNAL
(Condensed)

Date	Detail	General Ledger Dr.	General Ledger Cr.	Bank Dr.	Bank Cr.	Names	Accounts Payable Dr.	Accounts Payable Cr.	Purch. Dr.	Sales. Cr.	Names	Accounts Receivable Dr.	Accounts Receivable Cr.
7	Payroll W/E Jan. 6												
	Wages	2152			1638						H. Weaver	190	
	Inc. tax		425								B. Little	254	
	C.P.P.		33							763	D. Frances	319	415
	U.I.C.		40							16			319
											P. Buckle	624	
	H. Blandford (rent)	500		734	487	Wheeler & Company	487	268	268	723	D. Frances	50	
	Car expense	112			56	Sign-Ad Co.	56				L. Woods	49	
	Bldg. repairs	64			500	Reliable Motors Inc.	96	112			N. Devlin		
	Bank Loan	200			96	Hoover Co.		64			P. Gower		
	Petty Cash	75			200								
					75								
	and so on, to the end of the month.												
		11693	2172	12670	13474		4117	3920	3756	13481		13481	12670

97

Journal. If it gets still larger, you should pull out the Credit Accounts Payable column and start a separate journal for purchases and expenses.

c. BANK COLUMNS

These are also covered in the receivables and payables chapters, but there is one confusing point we might deal with here: when you lean over the counter and ask the clerk what your balance is, he or she tells you that you have a "credit" balance of $500. On *your* books this is a *debit* balance.

You can keep straight on this if you remember that when you make a deposit you charge the bank just as if you had delivered goods instead of money.

Things are the other way around if you have an overdraft. Then, on your books, the bank has a credit balance like any other creditor.

But for further comment on the bank and its columns, see the chapter on "The Bank and You."

d. ODDS AND ENDS

There are a few more things you should know about the synoptic journal. They are put down here, not necessarily in order of importance, but to get them out of the way so we can get on to the next chapter.

1. If you need more than one page for the month, total the columns of each page as you go along, and, *if you are sure they cross-balance*, carry the total of each column to the top of the same column on the next page. If you are in a hurry and want to get all the entries written in before cross-balancing, that's all right, go right ahead with pages two and three, but leave a blank line at the head of each page so you will have room to put down your "carried forward" totals. If you forget this it means you will have to squeeze the carried forward figures in with a regular entry, and squeezed figures can be misread all too easily.

2. Use the "description" space on the left-hand side of the journal freely. Put in dates, names, invoice numbers and cheque numbers. This saves hunting for details later on.

3. Take all the space you need. Paper was made for people, not people for paper.

4. Keep your figures within the ruled vertical lines. Figures that spill over the lines are hard to add correctly.

5. If you make a mistake and enter either the wrong figures in the right column, or the right figures in the wrong column, correct it by running your pen through the error. *Don't use ink eraser.* This is standard accounting procedure based on the theory that it is better to see and know why a mistake was made than not see and suspect the worse.

If you are in the right column with wrong figures, squeeze the right ones in just above the ones you have stroked out.

(Pencil can be used on primary records such as cash sheets. These are often subject to adjustment at the time they are made out, hence erasures don't matter.)

Now take another look at the sample synoptic pages. Simple, aren't they? Gives you a complete picture of what went on during the month's business.

As for what went on in the preceding months, you can read all about it in the next chapter.

8

THE GENERAL LEDGER

An expression that your accountant frequently uses is "the general ledger." He may appear to toss the phrase about with abandon but, if you listen carefully, you will detect an undertone of respect. I don't mean that he stands in awe of the ledger, but rather that his feelings are like those of a banker when the topic is liquid funds, or a lawyer when the subject of the constitution comes up. Familiarity, yes, but condescension, never.

This is because the general ledger contains the life history of a business, and in the long run accounting is neither more nor less than the accurate recording of business history.

That is why nearly all bookkeeping textbooks start out with the general ledger in the first chapter. The authors feel it is too vital to be ignored, even temporarily.

Fortunately for you, this is not a textbook on bookkeeping (although at times it may sound suspiciously like one) so you have been able to work up to the ledger the way you would if you were a bookkeeper writing up a set of books, and that is as the last thing to be reckoned with.

The general ledger is the final resting place for all the figures in your journals. It is a statistical storage cupboard, with the earliest figures at the bottom and the subsequent years stacked, shelf by shelf, above them.

The first figures in the ledger are your "Opening Entries." Your accountant worked them out after he got from you the details of how you started up your business. The opening entries are important, as you will remember from the chapter "On Buying a Business," and for that reason it is best to have a professional accountant make them, no matter how good you may consider yourself as a bookkeeper.

If you had started business by depositing a round sum of money in the bank and then proceeded immediately to buy goods for resale, the opening entry would be simple. It would be a debit to "Bank" and a credit to "Capital."

Even if your beginnings were as simple as that, the chances are that you had to buy some fixtures, furniture, or equipment right away, and those transactions should also be treated as a part of your opening entries.

It is even more likely that you purchased all or part of a going concern and that the deal was accompanied by all the palaver described in chapter 2. At any rate, your accountant will want to look at every document you signed, because from them he will build up his opening debits and credits, strictly on a "party that gives" and the "party that gets" basis.

For instance, when you bought the Jones Pickle Works in chapter 2, the opening entries would be like this:

Dr. Land	$ 8 000.00
Dr. Buildings	32 000.00
Dr. Merchandise inventory	13 852.00
Dr. 1½ ton truck	3 600.00
Dr. 1 showcase	1 800.00
Dr. 1 scales	600.00
Dr. Goodwill	148.00
	$60 000.00
Cr. You, capital	$20 000.00
Cr. Agreement for sale, payable	40 000.00
	$60 000.00

Your accountant would head up a page in the general ledger for each of the above titles, and in each he would enter the appropriate debit or credit. With the exception of the

Agreement for sale, payable, which will be paid off within a few years (you hope), all of those accounts will stay in the ledger for the life of your business. Every time your accountant takes a trial balance (e.g., adds up the debit balances and the credit balances separately to see if the totals are equal), he will include those original accounts. It may be the balances will increase or decrease — you may add to or dispose of assets, and certainly your inventory will fluctuate from year to year — but those original accounts will always remain in the general ledger.

Once the opening entries are made, everything else follows in your ledger on a pay-as-you-go basis. Every column heading in the journals will have a corresponding account of the same name in the general ledger. (You may have *two* columns in the journal with the same heading, one for debits and the other for credits, but you need only *one* account in the ledger, into which both debits and credits are posted.)

In addition to accounts corresponding with column headings, you will also need accounts in which to put the individual entries from the catchall or General Ledger columns.

If at any time you acquire an asset which, because of its importance, deserves special mention and attention, it, too, is entitled to a general ledger account of its own. A truck, car, tractor, or refrigerator would fall into such a class. Of course, if you already have a general ledger account for, say, "Equipment" and your new asset can be considered as merely another piece of equipment, then it goes in the existing "Equipment" account without fanfare.

On the credit side, if at any time you assume a liability that, because of its amount, terms of purchase, or other reason, is different from an ordinary or trade account payable, it too gets the special treatment. In this class are the tax deductions collected from employees, sales taxes collected, and the unpaid balance on the purchase price of the business.

Entries in the general ledger accounts are *always from a journal*, either as a column total or as one of the individual items that make up the General Ledger column. This is the same principle you use in your receivables and payables ledgers, where, as you will remember, a control account will not work unless *all* entries go through a journal first.

Posting from a journal to the general ledger is your assurance that the dollar totals of the debit and credit entries are equal.

If you made entries in it whenever you felt like it, without regard to equality of debits and credits, you wouldn't have a general ledger — you would have a book with a miscellaneous collection of business figures in it.

We talked a few paragraphs back about opening general ledger accounts for assets bought or liabilities assumed.

When the reverse happens (i.e., you sell an asset or pay all or part of a liability), your credit or debit entry naturally goes in the same account.

This is simple enough when you are paying off a liability — the debit either reduces or wipes out the creditor's balance. When you sell an asset, however, a nasty little exception arises and its name is Depreciation.

If the asset is something you have owned for along time, the chances are it has been written down (depreciated) to allow for decline in value through wear and tear. Therefore, while the asset may be sitting in its ledger account at the original price you paid for it, in another part of the ledger is an account called "Reserve for Depreciation," (or "Accumulated Depreciation," "Provision for Depreciation," etc.) which says, in effect, "No, not so!" As a result of this second account, the present *net* value of the asset on your books is less than its original cost. It is less by exactly the amount that has been written off and stored in the Reserve for Depreciation.

I mention this so you will realize the necessity of going slow. By all means, sell the asset if you can get a good price for it, and put through an entry in your cash journal like this:
Dr. Cash (or Bank, if you deposit the money right away)
    Cr. Sale of Automatic Brisket Cutter

and put the credit entry in the General Ledger column. Then, if you have read the part about depreciation, until you can repeat it backwards in your sleep, you may make the general ledger entries that are necessary. Otherwise, let your accountant make them.

a.   EVERY DEBIT HAS ITS CREDIT

By now it should be clear that no matter how many batches of entries are made from your journal or journals to the general ledger, if they have been made correctly, the sum of the debit balances in the general ledger will always be equal to the sum of the credit balances.

For, consider this:

> — The debits and credits in your opening entries were equal.
> — The debits and credits from your journals are equal.
> — Therefore, if you combine the two sets in the general ledger the new debit and credit balances must also be equal.

You will notice that I said "combine" and not "add," and for good reason. You can add a debit to a debit, or a credit to a credit, but you cannot add debit and credit dollars any more than you can add apples and oranges.

You match them, dollar for dollar, and the one with the most dollars wins.

For instance, if the balance in the general ledger Bank account is a debit at the end of June, and you have just posted (entered) a larger amount to the credit side of the account (from the foot of the Cr. Bank column in the cash journal), your new balance in the Bank account will be a credit.

The ledger page might look like this:

BANK

Date 19-	Description	Folio	Debits	Credits	Dr. or Cr.	Balance
May	bal. forward		179.00		Dr.	179.00
June		C6		372.00	Cr.	193.00
June		C6	316.00		Dr.	123.00
July		C7		357.00	Cr.	234.00

You then post the figure of $408 from the foot of the debit column, and your balance at the end of July will be Dr. $174.

Most bookkeepers, to save space, put debit and credit entries from the same journal on the same line in the ledger account, so that the above would appear like this:

Date 19-			Dr.	Cr.		Balance
May	bal. forward		179.00		Dr.	179.00
June		C6	316.00	372.00	Dr.	123.00
July		C7	408.00	357.00	Dr.	174.00

Notice that when the May balance was carried forward from the bottom of the preceding ledger page, it was placed in the debit column, *as well as* in the balance column.

This is done so that at all times the difference between the totals of the debit and credit columns on the page will equal the latest balance. This bit of arithmetic is known as "proving the page," and it wouldn't work if you left out your carry-forward figure from the top of the debit or credit column.

The figures in the folio column tell you where each entry came from. Thus, "C6" means "Cash Book, page 6," and "PJ7" would stand for "Purchase Journal, page 7."

It is highly recommended that you carry this idea further: every time you make an entry in one of your journals, you write the appropriate folio reference number on one corner of the cheque stub, purchase invoice, sales invoice, or whatever.

Not only will this show that the voucher has been "journalized," it will also give you a water-tight cross-reference system, something that can save you a lot of hasty hunting and page turning later on.

Posting debits and credits to the general ledger is like throwing weights on a pair of scales, with pans for debits on the left and for credits on the right.

You begin with the starting balance, shovel in a debit or a credit, and then read the scales to see which side is heavier. At the end of the month, when you have finished shovelling, weights should be equal on both sides. If they aren't, you've either put a debit or a credit on the wrong pan, or else made an error in arithmetic or in copying.

The general ledger can be a useful tool around the office. When you look at the balances in the accounts you can see at a glance the values of what you own, the money you owe, the revenue you have earned, and the expenses you have been put to. At your year-end (or sooner if need be) your accountant will clear out all the revenue and expense accounts and transfer the difference, as a profit or loss, to your capital account.

b. YOUR FISCAL YEAR-END

Your year-end does not necessarily mean December 31. You have the choice, from an income tax point of view, of ending your business year at any time between January 1 and December 31. (A month-end is best, because split months mean a lot of extra work.)

However, once you have decided on the date, you must stick to it for subsequent years.

Your fiscal year should end when your business is at its lowest seasonal ebb. This results in less inventory to count and, because there are fewest accounts outstanding, less chance of inaccurate receivables and payables figures.

You should, however, give very serious thought to ending your business year sometime between May and November inclusive, regardless of when your seasonal low point occurs. This is because 90% of businesses have December 31 as their year-end, and between that time and the income tax deadline your accountant works evenings and weekends until his endurance is stretched to the snapping point. All work goes through his office fast, he works under constant tension, and he does not have time to give thought to any unusual problems, tax or otherwise, which may come up.

Therefore if he can close your books at some other time of the year, not only will he bless you, but he will be able to give you more value for your accounting dollar.

c. DEPRECIATION

Depreciation is the accountant's way of saying write-off. This is just as much an expense as rent, light, advertising, or anything else that adds to the cost of doing business. Depreciation is the cost of your fixed assets, such as buildings, machinery, fixtures and heavy equipment, but because these things wear out slowly, the cost must be spread over a number of years.

The question of just how long these assets will last has been the subject of many a disagreement between borrowers and credit-granting institutions. Over the years, however, a list of acceptable write-off rates has been compiled, and if you stick to this list (your accountant has it) you are not likely to get into arguments with the bank.

Even so, at best, depreciation is nothing more than an intelligent guess, and as you probably know, accountants hate making guesses, intelligent or otherwise.

The ideal fixed asset, from your accountant's point of view, would carry a special warranty from the manufacturer. It would consist of an ironclad guarantee that after a specified number of years the asset would wear out. Buildings, for instance, would be so constructed that after exactly 40 years the walls would fall like those of Jericho, while machinery, at the end of 10 years, would automatically fly apart into little pieces, like the one-hoss shay.

Then your accountant would no longer have to estimate depreciation rates; he would *know*.

Accountants, however, have long since resigned themselves to an imperfect world, where equipment performs merrily 10 years after it has been written off the books. To protect themselves they have devised a simple system whereby they can always tell from the books —

— the original cost of the asset,
— the amount of write-off to date,
— the remaining *net* book value of the asset.

With these three vital bits of information an accountant can make adjustments on the books necessitated by write-off rates which prove to be too high or too low.

Normally, depreciation entries are made once a year, when the operating accounts are closed and an income statement made up.

To illustrate, let's presume you bought a building for $40 000 and its life is estimated at 40 years. The write-off, then, will be 1/40 of $40 000 every year, e.g., $1 000 or 2½% of the cost of the asset. (This is known as "straight line" depreciation.)

The accounting entry will be:

Dr. Building Depreciation
 Expense $1 000.00
    Cr. Reserve for Depreciation
    (Building) $1 000.00

If you are in business at the same stand for 40 years (bored, perhaps, but still eating), at the end of that time your Reserve for Depreciation (Building) will have $40 000 in it,

108

equalling the cost of the building, and on your balance sheet the *net* value of the building will be zero. From then on you cannot charge up building depreciation as an expense.

The phrase "Reserve for Depreciation" is a much misunderstood expression, and no wonder, for like most accountant's reserves, a depreciation reserve is not a reserve. "Allowance" or "provision" for depreciation is much nearer the truth, but "reserve" is firmly established and changes in accounting language are slow.

The point to keep in mind is this: A reserve for depreciation does not mean that the money has been placed in a separate bank account to buy a new asset when the old one is worn out. If you did that, pretty soon you wouldn't have any money left in your regular bank account.

A reserve for depreciation is *strictly a bookkeeping convenience*. It is the accounting estimate of how much an asset has declined in value since its purchase.

However, to return to your building, it is likely that long before the 40 years are up you will have sold the building for either more or less than its net book value at the time.

Let's presume you sell it after five years of ownership. By that time you will have written off five times $1 000 and the balances in your general ledger accounts will be:

— Building		
(original cost)	(Dr.)	$40 000.00
— Reserve for Depreciation		
(Bldg.)	(Cr.)	5 000.00
leaving a net book value of	(Dr.)	$35 000.00

If you sell your building for more than the net book value, you will make a profit, and if for less, you will suffer a loss.

Looking at it from the optimistic side, let's say you have sold it for $60 000.00

The accounting entry would be:

Dr. Cash $60 000.00
Dr. Reserve for
Depreciation (Building) 5 000.00
    Cr. Building (original cost) $40 000.00
    Cr. profit on sale
    of building 25 000.00

and, on analysis, you will find the entry entirely logical.

Thus, it —

(a) records the receipt of the sale price,

(b) takes the accumulated depreciation out of your books — for since you no longer have a building you no longer need a reserve,

(c) removes the building from your books for the same reason,

(d) give you your net book profit on the deal.

To look at the deal from the pessimist's point of view, let's say you sold your building for $30 000.

The accounting entry would be:

Dr. Cash $30 000.00
Dr. Reserve for Depreciation
(Building) 5 000.00
Dr. Loss on sale 5 000.00
    Cr. Building (original cost) $40 000.00

and, on analysis, you will find this entry just as logical as the first.

d. CAPITAL COST ALLOWANCES

Many years ago the tax department imposed its own ground rules for taking depreciation and, in fact, for income tax purposes depreciation is called "capital cost allowance."

Taxwise it works out as a sort of rolling readjustment of book values, whereby you start with your original assets, add

110

the cost of any new ones, deduct the proceeds of any disposals or trade-ins, and "claim" a percentage of the remaining balance. A minor complication arises because the tax department, always chasing that extra dollar, says you may take only half the regular rate of write-off on assets acquired during your current fiscal year.

To illustrate, let us look at a common situation. You have been in business for several years and you own a delivery truck which is shown on your last year's tax return as written down to $7 140. This year you bought a new truck for $10 000, less a trade-in allowance of $6 000. Your capital cost allowance calculation would be as follows:

Truck, forward from last year		$7 140.00
Add: cost of new truck	$10 000.00	
Less: old truck traded in	6 000.00	
Net cost of new truck		4 000.00
sub-total		11 140.00

At this stage you have a mixed figure; the top part you can write off at 30%, but the remaining $4 000 has to be at 15%. To simplify the arithmetic and to produce a figure wholly subject to the 30% rate, you deduct half the net cost

of the new asset, thus	2 000.00
giving you an "adjusted balance" of	9 140.00
which can properly be written off at 30%, thus	2 742.00
leaving you a year-end balance of	$6 398.00

to carry forward to next year's tax return, where, unless you persist in buying another truck, it can be written down at 30% without complications. This year-end figure is known technically as your "undepreciated capital cost," which is tax double-speak for "net book value."

You should keep in mind that you, or your accountant, create these figures to please the tax department, and that the actual values on your own books may be very different.

You may be pleased to learn that, provided you are in business for a full 12 months, it doesn't matter *when* you buy or sell your assets as long as it is within the 12-month period. You can buy a new truck on the last day of your business year and, subject to the 50% reduction mentioned above, you can still swing it into the total on which you may claim your maximum permissible allowance. But don't persuade yourself (as many people do) that you will *make* money by buying a truck or car on the last day of your fiscal year. Assets wear out, your money is tied up, and your only immediate gain is to put off some of your income tax for some of the time.

The write-off basis illustrated is applied to all your depreciable assets and your accountant can tell you the different rates for the different "classes" of assets.

There is one important catch to the tax department's rules. If, eventually, you sell all your assets and get more than their written-down value, you run into "recapture of depreciation." In effect, the tax department says: "The amount we allowed you for wear and tear obviously wasn't needed, so now we'll put it back into your income." And they do.

As might be expected, people who contemplate disposing of assets they have depreciated over a long period are anxious to know if there are ways of avoiding "recapture."

Well, there are various ways, although not all of them appeal to or are available to the average taxpayer.

If you and the buyer agree in writing, at the time of the sale, that your assets are not worth any more than the amounts you have written them down to for tax purposes, then there is no recapture. In fact, assuming there are reasonable grounds for it, if you can get the buyer to agree that your assets are worth even less, then you are entitled to a final bit of depreciation called "terminal allowance."

Unfortunately for you, nowadays most buyers have an accountant at their elbow who keeps whispering, "Make them agree to a high asset figure so we can take plenty of depreciation."

This situation comes about when the deal involves a mixture of things such as land, which cannot be depreciated, and equipment, buildings, automobiles, and the like, which can be depreciated at lush rates.

If a stalemate ensues and a deal is made without agreement on how many dollars for which asset, the tax department (for income tax purposes) will decide the issue for you. Needless to say, that decision will lean toward recapture.

A simpler way to avoid recapture on sale of your assets is to buy another group of assets before your taxation year is up. Even if there is a gap when you own none, provided you watch your deadline dates and provided the replacement assets belong to the same "class," you can swing from one group to another without running into tax. You will still, however, only be putting off the evil day because your new assets have to be fitted in with the rolling readjustment mentioned before, and you cannot claim on what they actually cost you. You start where you left off, with the same recapture problem hanging over your head.

If you own an apartment or other revenue property, the most pleasant method of all may come your way. To your surprise, one day a real estate company makes you a handsome offer for your property and they tell you they are not interested in the building because they will promptly tear it down and erect a super-building. In other words, all they want is the land.

At this point, if you have definitely decided to sell, two courses are open to you:

(a) If you sell without further ado and at the same time obtain a letter or other document from the buyers signifying they are buying the land only, the tax department (up until this writing) will not insist on recapture of deprecation previously taken.

(b) If you tear down your building (on the not-always-safe assumption that you have a sure sale), you can then sell your property as bare land and take a substantial "terminal allowance." This gives you a large slice of tax-free income.

It must be emphasized at this point that the sale of your old property should be fortuitous. You must be prepared to prove that your intentions were honorable and that your heart is pure. If you bought a revenue property, knowing full well that in a few years it could be resold as land, then not only would you face recaptured depreciation but also regular tax on your profit on the sale of land.

From your point of view it is best that elimination of recapturable depreciation, like capital gain, should happen obviously by accident.

Which leads to the questions: "To depreciate or not to depreciate?"

Right away let's concede that assets that wear out rapidly, such as trucks, cars, tools, digging equipment and all the machines which receive a battering from normal usage, should be depreciated (if you have income to kill) as fast as tax regulations permit. After all, depreciation is supposed to represent wear and tear, and with a host of items it certainly takes place.

The area for debate surrounds those assets that last a long time, mainly buildings, where often the allowable rates are much in excess of the actual decline in value that takes place, if it takes place at all.

To take in the whole field, let us assemble first of all the arguments in favor of taking depreciation:

(a) Because you may claim from zero up to the maximum percentage in each class, it is the most flexible way to adjust your taxable income. Take what you need to offset income, but no more than the amount required.

(b) Often it reduces or eliminates tax at a time when you are scrambling for every dollar you can lay your hands on (to pay for the assets you are depreciating).

(c) Depreciation from one business may give you an artificial loss, which you can set against profits from another business, thereby lowering your over-all taxable income.

(d) You have temporary use of the money you save. You can invest this and earn interest, or pay off debts and save interest.

(e) Most people adopt the motto, "Who can read the future, so why pay tax when you don't have to?"

The arguments against taking depreciation run along these lines:

(a) If you know you are going to sell your asset for as much or more than you paid for it, you are going to run into recapture, so why not grit your teeth and pay tax as you go along, rather than have it hanging over your head, payable at some future date.

(b) As an extension of (a), if you pay tax now, it may be a moderate rate. If you put it off until you are clobbered with recapture, at that time your tax bracket may shoot up sky-high.

Despite the risk or prospect of paying at a high rate later, most people elect to take as much depreciation as they need in the here-and-now. They reason, with considerable logic, that if they sell their assets and run into recapture, at least

115

they will have the money with which to pay the tax. They are willing to take a chance on ending up in a high bracket.

To add to this swirl of confusion, the government of this country has the disconcerting habit of jiggling allowable depreciation rates up and down and varying the periods for which depreciation can be taken, depending on whether it thinks the economy needs cooling off or heating up.

Because of all these things, a little ignorance on your part could turn out to be very expensive at some future date. So, at his point in your pondering, I urge you to set up a candid and down-to-earth conference with your accountant.

He runs into depreciation problems all the time, he gets bulletins on all the changes and he knows what can be done to guard against future shock.

Together you can plan your best tax depreciation policy and please, no matter how many "good friends" you may have, don't let anybody give you amateur tax advice.

9
EXPENSES

An expense is an expense is an expense (to adapt Gertrude Stein's words), but this sentence is wrong in fact as well as in syntax.

Expenses are what prevent you from making so much money that the government will take most of it away from you in taxes. Expenses are sales to the people you buy from, and they are as much interested in high sales as you are in low expenses. This difference of viewpoint is known as "the free play of economic forces" or, alternatively, "cut-throat competition," depending on whether you are buying or selling.

Seriously, though, there are certain aspects of expenses to which much thought should be given.

To begin with, there are two reasons why you must break up and classify your expenses, rather than take the easy way and lump them together.

First, it gives you, the management, some idea of where your money has gone, what for, and whether any expenses are out of line.

Second, it shows the tax department in detail why you aren't making a fortune, and enables them to compare your expenses with those of others in the same line of business.

This means that your operating expenses should be broken down into 10 or more classes. Over the years the names of these basic expenses have tended to become standardized.

They are —

Accounting
Advertising
Bad debts
Freight and cartage
Fuel
Insurance
Interest and bank charges
Laundry (uniforms, overalls, etc.)
Legal and audit
Licences and permits
Light and power
Maintenance and repairs
Miscellaneous
Office
Operating supplies (wrapping paper, boxes, etc.)
Pension plan
Renewals and replacements
Rent
Stamps and stationery
Subscriptions and trade association dues
Telephone and telegraph
Travel
Truck or car operating
Unemployment insurance
Wages
Workers' Compensation

You can combine some of these if you like. "Accounting" is often grouped with "office," or "stamps and stationery." "Light and power" is often put with "Fuel" or with "Telephone and telegraph." The more expenses you show separately, however, the more the tax assessor is likely to conclude that you are a conscientious and painstaking individual and that all your figures are probably correct.

You should remember this important fact:

It is not enough for your expenses to be reasonable: *They must also look reasonable.*

Therefore you must resist the temptation to dump all sorts of hard-to-classify expenses into "Miscellaneous" or "General." Broadly speaking, Miscellaneous shouldn't run to more than 5% of your total expenses. Nothing irritates a tax assessor more than the sight of —

Miscellaneous expenses	$1 247.39
among a list of expenses totalling, say	5 013.47

He or she knows from experience that nine times out of ten it will consist of an innocuous collection of items such as painting, minor repairs, gas and oil bills, and a lot of etceteras. The tenth time it will include a questionable item such as wages paid to someone who doesn't want it reported, the cost of that trip to Toronto which wasn't really a business expense, or perhaps, a piece of equipment which should have been capitalized. This tenth time is what the tax assessor is paid to investigate, and you may be quite sure he or she will do it if only to break the monotony of the job.

The same rule applies to any expense account that can be used to cover up questionable items. Your "Repairs and Maintenance" expense for the year may have been very heavy, perhaps 25% of your total expenses, and all of it perfectly proper and legitimate. Nevertheless, *break it up*. Subdivide it like this:

Repairs and maintenance:	
Building reinforcement	$ 406.96
New linoleum	600.00
Plumbing	550.00
Furnace repairs	296.00
Painting contract	750.00
	$2 602.96

By the same token try to avoid expense names that are too vague, such as "Store Expense," "Sales Expense" or

119

"Buying Expense." They mean anything or nothing, and the tax assessor likes things definite.

You might as well save yourself and your accountant time and money in the first place by splitting these coverall titles into specific expenses while the details are fresh in your memory. If you don't, you may have to do it later with the tax department looking over your shoulder.

So much for expense in general. Now let's deal with a few specific expenses that deserve comment.

a. ADVERTISING

The bulk of this will be for advertisements placed in publications, sign painting, electric sign rentals and the like. In addition, but within reasonable limits, you may include expenditures made to promote business. If you contribute $25 toward instruments for the high-school band, it may not be because you are a music lover. It may be that if you don't contribute, it will be mighty poor advertising. So instead of listing it under "p" for "pressure," you may properly, although in a negative way, put it under "Advertising Expenses."

b. CAR AND TRUCK EXPENSES

Here again if you have a relatively large amount, the breakdown rule applies. Show gas and oil separately from repairs, and if you operate a number of vehicles, the cost of tires, insurance and licences. Of course, if you have one car and use it only part of the time for business, one total will probably do.

Another thing, if you travel around the country extensively on selling trips, for goodness' sakes buy gas on a credit card. Nothing gets lost more quickly than a receipt from a country gas station, not to mention the nuisance of tallying the ones you don't lose.

If you use your car for personal as well as business use, for tax purposes you may only claim the portion of costs due to business use. The easiest way to handle this is to put all car expenses through the books and then have your accountant make one adjusting entry at your year-end. (Or buy two cars, one for business use exclusively.)

c. ENTERTAINMENT

This a perfectly legitimate expense if incurred in connection with business, but, just the same, don't indulge in it too heavily.

The reason is that to a tax assessor the word suggests cases of liquor and squads of starlets. Nothing may be further from the truth, but, nevertheless, the word has had a faint smell since the days of the Romans.

To counteract this, it is advisable to keep a fairly detailed memo record of your promotional expenses, with dates, amounts and circumstances to back up your figures. The test the tax assessor will apply is whether the amount is reasonable in the light of custom in your trade.

d. INSURANCE

If this is a small amount, never mind dividing up the three-year fire premiums into thirds. If, however, your insurance is very substantial, give your accountant a list of the policies you hold, together with the following information:

— Annual premium of each policy
— Beginning date and expiry date of each policy

With this he can work out how much of your insurance expense should be transferred to "Deferred Charges" on your balance sheet.

e. INTEREST AND BANK CHARGES

If only the bank were involved, this would be simple. Banks charge overdraft, loan interest, and service charges against your account every month on your statement where you can see it.

A difficulty arises when you have been making payments on a mortgage or an agreement of sale, and the payments are a flat sum per month, principal and interest combined. The question is: how much of the amount paid is interest?

If you are dealing with a mortgage company or realtor, the chances are they will give you a statement at the end of the year with this information on it.

If, however, you are dealing with an individual, probably he or she hasn't the vaguest idea as to how much principal remains unpaid. This means that you (or, more often, an accountant) must sit down and make out a table like the one in Sample #20.

The example is a six months' table whereas yours will probably run for twelve months. And, unless you have a set of interest tables, there is no alternative except to figure out the interest (on the first payment, for instance) like this:

$$\$\,2\,500 \ \times \ \frac{9}{100} \ \times \ \frac{31}{365} \ = \ \$19.11$$

It is a dreary, monotonous bit of arithmetic, and for that reason I suggest you leave it to your accountant as he very likely has a set of interest tables or, more likely, an electronic calculator. However, if you insist on doing it yourself, you can check the accuracy of some of your calculations at least. The totals of the "interest paid" and the "principal paid" columns must, of course, equal the total "amount paid" column. Further, the principal you start out with (upper left-hand corner) *less* the "principal paid" total must equal the principal you still owe at the end (lower right-hand corner).

**SCHEDULE OF PAYMENTS OF INTEREST
AND PRINCIPAL**

(Rate of interest — 9%)
made by Joe Spiff against mortgage
held by K. Weaver

PRINCIPAL	DATE PAID	NUMBER OF DAYS OUTSTANDING	AMOUNT PAID	INTEREST PAID	PRINCIPAL PAID	PRINCIPAL REMAINING UNPAID
2500.00	Feb. 1	31	50.00	19.11	30.89	2469.11
2469.11	March 1	28	50.00	17.05	32.95	2436.16
2436.16	April 1	31	50.00	18.62	31.38	2404.78
2404.78	May 1	30	50.00	17.79	32.21	2372.57
2372.57	June 1	31	50.00	18.13	31.87	2340.70
2340.70	July 1	30	50.00	17.31	32.69	2308.01
			300.00	108.01	191.99	

And here is a tip if you are doing a 12-month schedule: put in lightly penciled subtotals every three months and use them for the above-mentioned checks. If you complete the whole works and then, on checking, find you have made an error in line four, all your interest calculations from line four down will have to be done again. (At this point most people put it aside for their accountant to finish.)

But to end this subsection on a cheerful note, nowadays you can have a computer centre print out a complete schedule of principal and interest covering the entire life of the mortgage. The computer does this in a few seconds, and for most people it is well worth the small charge involved.

f. OPERATING SUPPLIES

Normally there are no complications about this, but sometimes you may end up your year with a lot of wrapping paper, twine, stationery, boxes, or crates on hand. These supplies have definitely not been used up and so, strictly speaking, what they cost you is not an expense any more than your stock of unsold merchandise is an expense. If you inventory them and give the figure to your accountant, he will make the necessary adjustment on the books with an entry like this:

Dr. Inventory of supplies on hand $900.00

    Cr. Operating supplies expense $900.00

The inventory figure will then appear on your balance sheet either as a current asset or under the "Deferred Charges" group depending on what books your accountant studied when he was training.

Don't bother with this if the amount involved is small or if it isn't apt to change much from year to year. If it is a large figure or the amount fluctuates widely, then for accuracy you should take it into account.

g. STATIONERY

Your letterheads, billheads, envelopes, etc. come under this category, as also do accounting supplies such as journals, ledger and ledger pages, and I would suggest you let your accountant select your accounting stationery.

If, however, you buy these latter items yourself, do NOT buy

— bound ledgers,
— ledger leaves with debit and credit columns only.

The bound ledger is a carry-over from the last century and should have been left there. You come to the bottom of a page and find that the succeeding page is already in use, so you have to carry forward your balance from page 20 to page 63. After a while, the resulting jumble of accounts gets too irritating to bear, so your accountant buys a loose-leaf ledger (loose only in the sense that pages can be removed or inserted easily), which is what you should have got in the first place.

Ledger leaves with debit and credit columns but no balance columns went out with the horse, and if you buy any the salesperson will get a special bonus for getting rid of pre-war stock.

h. SHOP CAR EXPENSE

This expense is peculiar to service stations and garages. When you put 40 litres of gas in the shop car, how does it go on the books?

The easiest way is to ignore the transaction temporarily, but to keep a memo record of not only gas, but also parts, tires, and any other maintenance costs. Then, at your year-end, your accountant can put through one entry to cover the works, like this:

Dr. Shop car expense	$2 000.00	
Cr. Gas sales		$1 200.00
Cr. Purchases of parts		400.00
Cr. Purchases of tires		400.00

i. WAGES

This is usually the largest expense next to purchases. The figure on your year-end statement is gross wages, that is, wages before income tax, unemployment insurance, or any other deductions. On your cash sheets, if you pay your help in cash, the figure that appears will be net wages after deductions. For details on this sometimes confusing set-up, see the chapter on payrolls.

Money you take out of the business for your own use is *not* wages (nor is it necessarily profits). Even if you draw it regularly on the same day you pay your help, it is still not wages, but "Drawings." If this confuses you, think of it like this: your business is one of your personal belongings. If you transfer cash from the till to your pocket, you are neither richer nor poorer than before. Therefore, taking money out of your business is no more of an expense than shifting money from one pocket to another.

If you are running an incorporated company, then it is a different story. A company has a separate legal existence all its own whether you own all the shares or not. If you own an incorporated company and work for it, your wages are just as much an expense as anybody else's, and, furthermore, you will pay personal income tax on them. If, after you have drawn your wages, the company makes a profit, it will pay income tax on that profit at corporation rates. Again, if there is anything left after the company has paid its tax and you decide to draw it out as a dividend, you will pay income tax on the dividend.

This is the main reason why many small-business people choose not to incorporate.

j. INCOME TAXES

It may pain you to learn that income tax is not one of the expenses of doing business. You may, if you wish, treat it as an expense on your books, but be sure that it is left out of your calculations when you make up your tax returns. Properly speaking, it is a sharing of your profit with the government. A one-sided arrangement, true, but I doubt if you can change it.

Income tax is a complicated and devious subject that you will do well to leave in the hands of your accountant. It is one of his specialties, and if he is worth his salt he will take professional delight in making sure that you don't pay a nickel more than you have to. There is nothing illegal or immoral about this. It is just good, clean business.

There are other expenses not detailed above which may loom large among your pay-outs. Every business that requires special equipment is likely to have special expenses. Call such expenses by whatever name best describes them and show them on your financial statements that way.

10

THE BANK AND YOU

From your accountant's point of view, your dealings with the bank are the most important part of your business. He may realize in an absent-minded sort of a way that you have to buy merchandise, and that, having bought it, you must try to sell it. He may even concede, somewhat reluctantly, that there are a few more important things in business than writing up records.

But when it comes to *his* business, your accountant loves your bank. Your bank statements (or passbook), your cheque stubs and cancelled cheques are the cornerstone around which he builds your business records. For cash may come and cash may go, but once you have paid a bill by cheque, immediately there exists a permanent written record for all the world to see. Receipted bills can and do disappear like snow in the spring, but for some reason people hang on to cancelled cheques as though they were sweepstakes tickets, for which habit your accountant is deeply grateful.

If you reach the stage where you write up the cash journal, you will soon realize for yourself the importance of bank records.

In the meantime, let's proceed on the assumption that your accountant is writing up your journals, and you are curious to know what he does.

The first thing *you* do is pick up your cancelled cheques from the bank shortly after the end of the month and put them in a safe place. If you want to look them over to make sure there are no forgeries, go right ahead, but *leave the cheques in the order in which you get them back from the bank.*

Your accountant may want to tick them off against the entries on the bank statement, and if you shuffle them it will take three times as long as if you had left them in their original order. And *please* never remove a cancelled cheque unless you put in a memo with complete details to replace it. Without the cheque or memo it will look to him as if the bank had done you in the eye, and if he is feeling that way, your accountant may even ring up the bank and tell them just that.

a. WRITING UP THOSE BANK TRANSACTIONS

So now, having sat down with the journal in front of him, your accountant proceeds to enter in the "Cr. Bank" column the amounts of the cheques from the stubs or your cheque book. If you have put on the stubs what the cheques are for, he knows what to charge the debits to. If you haven't, generally he can tell either by looking up the preceding months, or because he has lived long enough in your town he knows the names of most of your creditors and what they deal in.

If he doesn't know, he grumbles at your negligence and, if the cheque is a big one, telephones you to find out what it is for.

If the cheque is a small one, he may —

(a) telephone you anyway, or

(b) charge it to purchases as being the most likely account, or

(c) if he is pressed for time, charge it to your personal drawings account, and the heck with it.

Plainly, it is in your own interest to put full details on the cheque stubs.

Next, he looks over your bank statement and picks out items for which there are no cheques, such as overdraft interest, service charges, and the like. These he enters in the journals as if they were cheques.

He then adds up the deposits you have made during the month. He may do this from the carbon copies in your deposit book, or, more likely, from the deposit entries on your bank statements. If you are using cash sheets, he will try to tie his figure in with the deposits listed on your sheets. If it doesn't tie in, he will make a mental move to run down the difference later, and in the meantime, will use the actual total the bank has credited you with during the month. He will enter this in the journal as a debit to the "Bank" and a credit to "Cash."

Now he turns to the cancelled cheques themselves. Let us suppose he is writing up the month of March. First he looks through the cheques and sorts out any dated February or earlier. These are cheques that have been written up in your books in the previous month or months but which, for one reason or another, were not presented for payment until March.

He made out a list of these "outstanding" cheques when he wrote up the books for February, and now he ticks off the list any that have come in during March. Unless somebody is deliberately not cashing a cheque, they will likely all have come in.

Having dealt with old cheques, he now does the same thing with the current month's batch, but this time the list he uses is the column of the journal he has just written up.

Once again he will find that some of the cheques you have written have not been presented to the bank, and these are March cheques "outstanding." He makes a list of these and adds to them any cheques not crossed off the February list, and which are therefore still outstanding. This gives him the total of all cheques you have issued up to the end of March, but which have not yet been charged against your bank account.

b. RECONCILING THE BANK

Now he has the information he needs to "reconcile the bank," and this is how he does it.

He looks up the balance in "Bank" account in the general ledger as at the end of last month, i.e., February. This is the amount you should have left in your account if every cheque you had written had been presented to the bank and paid.

He finds the general ledger "Bank" account balance at the end of February is	$ 534.00
To this he adds the total of your March deposits as shown by your bank statement, viz.	<u>3 762.00</u>
making a subtotal of	4 296.00
From this he deducts the total of all the cheques you have written during the month, e.g., the figure at the foot of the "Cr. Bank" column	<u>3 894.00</u>
And thus he arrives at the "true" amount you would have in the bank if all your cheques had been presented, namely	402.00
but he knows that some of them have not come in yet, because a few minutes ago he made up a list of just those cheques, the total of which was	<u>177.00</u>
So if he adds back these unpresented cheques to your "true" bank balance he will then have your actual balance of	579.00
He glances at your bank statement, and lo and behold, it is	<u>564.00</u>
So, he mutters and starts to look for	<u>15.00</u>

There are about half a dozen places where he may have gone astray. He hunts down his difference step by step, as follows:

1. He goes over his additions in the journal, the list of outstanding cheques, and the total of the amounts deposited.

2. He scans the bank statement to see if he has missed a bank charge of some kind.

3. He goes through the cancelled cheques again to see if among them there are any items such as trade acceptances, drafts or notes, which he has omitted to write up in the cheque column in the journal.

4. He goes over the bank statement to see if the bank has certified or "marked" any cheques. If this has happened the bank will put the notation "CC" opposite the entry, and so far as you are concerned the cheque has been paid. But if the holder of the cheque hasn't cleared it through *his* bank, it will not be among the cancelled cheques, and your accountant may have inadvertently put it on the outstanding list.

5. He compares your cancelled cheques, one by one, with the entries on the bank statement, just to be sure that he and the bank agree about your threes and fives, or sevens and nines.

6. As a last resort he will check the arithmetic on the bank statement. About one in a million entries there will be a mistake on a machine-produced bank statement, and even that is likely to be through a pen and ink adjustment. If it is a passbook and the bank ledger is also handwritten, then the chances of a bank error are greater, perhaps one in a hundred thousand.

In the example we are working on your accountant found his difference was due to a certified cheque for $15. He had this cheque listed as outstanding, but on re-examining your bank statement he saw that it was certified by the bank on March 28, and that the bank clerk neglected to put a voucher (a slip of paper showing the amount of the cheque and the fact that it had been charged to your account) among the cancelled cheques. Thus, when he ticked off the cancelled cheques against the column in the journal, he missed it.

131

Accordingly, he changes the outstanding cheque total to $162 and makes out a reconciliation like this:

General Ledger Balance (Debit)		$402.00
Add: O/S Cheques	$27.00	
	19.00	
	54.00	
	30.00	
	32.00	<u>162.00</u>
Balance per bank statement		<u>$564.00</u>

Some accountants work from the bottom up, taking the bank statement balance, *less* outstanding cheques, to arrive at the general ledger "true" balance. It doesn't matter which way you do it. The point is, a bank reconciliation should show the statement balance and the ledger balance, and how they are linked together.

One more thing and we are through with the bank reconciliation. Sometimes your cash book column will include a deposit on the last day of the month, which, for some reason, wasn't put in the bank until the first day of the next month. This is known as an "outstanding deposit," and in your reconciliation it is handled exactly the same as an outstanding cheque, only in reverse. After you have added in your outstanding cheques to the general ledger bank balance, you *subtract* your outstanding deposit to arrive at your bank statement figure.

As to where bank reconciliations should go, opinions vary. Some accountants write them on the back of the bank statement itself, others on a sheet of paper which they keep in their files. The best and most frequently followed plan is to write the reconciliation somewhere in the journal itself, where it can't get lost.

On the subject of bank deposits, you may thing it unnecessary to say anything about such a simple business. Nevertheless, there's a right way and a wrong way to make up a deposit, and it's better to be right than sorry.

So:

— always keep a copy, preferably a carbon,
— always write in names (legibly) when you deposit cheques.

It is a good idea also, if you accept a cheque from a customer and it is not his or her own, to write the customer's name alongside the name of the person who wrote the cheque. (This is a must if you keep accounts receivable.) Otherwise if Ann Spiff gives you a cheque of Steve Wrykscki's in settlement of her (Ann's) account, when you come to write up your receivables you may wonder who Steve Wrykscki is and why he gave you a cheque. And if your accountant writes up your receivables, *he* certainly won't know.

There will be occasional deposits in your bank account that you do not make yourself, such as bank loans, drafts collected by the bank, bond coupons credited to your account, etc. Most banks will mail you a copy of the credit slip, and this should be fastened to a blank page in your deposit book. If there is no slip, make a notation on your bank statement (when you get it) stating the nature of the deposit.

Normally your accountant will spot irregular deposits of this kind, but not always. If he doesn't, there is the chance he may credit the (apparently) extra money to sales, so, to be safe, mark them plainly.

If you are writing up the synoptic or cash book yourself, make sure the total at the foot of the "Dr. Bank" column ties in with the total of the deposits shown on your bank statement.

If it doesn't agree, it may be due to an outstanding deposit, in which case you show it on your reconciliation. If the difference is due to a loan, draft collected, etc., as described above, put the necessary debit or debits in the "Dr. Bank" column and the balancing entry or entries in whatever credit columns is indicated.

Your "Dr. Bank" column total should then be the same as the figure for deposits or your bank reconciliation.

NSF CHEQUES — These were discussed in the "Cash" chapter, but they are enough of a nuisance to warrant mentioning again. Basically, it is a question of whether they will be made good or not.

If the bounce is purely temporary, deposit the cheque again, *by itself*, and mark plainly on the deposit slip, "Redeposit."

If the bounce is of unknown duration, the accounting treatment depends on whether you are running on a cash basis, or on an accrual basis.

If the former, your accountant will make the entry "Cr. Bank" and "Dr. Sales" just as if you had issued a cheque for a refund.

If the latter, your accountant will make the entry "Cr. Bank" and "Dr. Accounts Receivable" just as if it were an invoice or sale of goods.

Watch for this if you run a daily cash sheet. If you pick up, say, a $40 NSF cheque from the bank, collect $40 cash from the customer, and then deposit $40 along with your other cash without any comment, your accountant will wonder where the extra $40 came from.

So:

> — when on a cash basis, show the cheque (or the currency that replaces it) as revenue cash (Sales),
> — when on an accrual basis, show the cheque (or the currency that replaces it) as non-revenue cash (Accounts Receivable Collected).

Then your cash sheet figure will offset your accountant's journal entry and your cash records will be straight.

And that concludes the mechanics of your bookkeeping relations with the bank.

11
PAYROLLS

a. DEDUCTIONS

Once upon a time if you opened an arithmetic book you would find a problem like this: "John works in Mrs. Brown's store. He earns 25 cents an hour and works eight hours a day for six days a week. How much money does he take home every Saturday night?" The answer in the back of the book would be $12, and probably John figured he had a pretty good job.

Nowadays, John might be willing to work for $80 a day (temporarily, of course), but if he expected to take home $400 on payday, he would get an awful shock.

Taxing authorities discovered some time ago that they can collect the most money with the least fuss by standing in the line alongside John on payday. The biggest deduction is usually for employees' income tax. After that there is unemployment insurance, the Canada Pension Plan, and possibly other deductions made at either John's or his union's request.

Let us take John, for instance, and put him through the wringer. He made $400 last week, gross wages. From that was deducted:

Income tax	$ 75.00
Canada Pension Plan	6.00
Union dues	3.00
Savings bond	10.00
Unemployment insurance	9.00
Cash advances	20.00
Hospital insurance premium	4.00
Total deductions	$127.00

135

On some of these deductions, John has no say in the matter. Others, such as cash advances and savings bonds, are up to him.

b. PAYROLL BOOKS

As John's employer, you must keep track of all these things, and the best way is to use a payroll book.

Payroll books (often called time books) come in various shapes and sizes at various prices. Don't try to economize by getting a small one. Spend a dollar or two at the nearest stationery store and get one that has a lot of columns for deductions and adequate space in the figure columns.

There is nothing complicated about a payroll book — you just fill in the columns from left to right. Start with gross wages, take off the deductions, and end up with take-home pay. If you have more than one employee, do the same for each, line by line, and when you've written in the last figure, draw a line across the page. Add up each column and put in each total. "Prove" the sheet by cross balancing it, i.e., *total* gross wages, less *total* deductions, must equal *total* take-home pay. (Look at Sample #21.)

You can get payroll books for weekly, biweekly, semi-monthly and monthly pay-periods. If you pay by the week and the month-end comes in the middle of a week, for tax deduction purposes use the last payday in the month as your cutoff date.

You can pay your employees

— by cash out of the till (it goes under "net wages" on your cash sheet),
— by individual cheques
— by one cheque made out for the exact amount of the total take-home pay and cashed for that purpose only.

TIME, Week ending _____ 19 ___

Name	Sun.	Mon.	Tues.	Wed.	Thurs.	Fri.	Sat.	Total time	Rate per hr. or day	Total earnings	Tax	CPP	UIC	Other	Total Deductions	Net Amount due	Signature or cheque no.
													Deductions				
J. Shields	X	X	8	8	8	8	8	40	12	480	89	11	14		114	366	
H. Burke	X	8	8	8	X	8	8	40	9	360	53	8	11		72	288	
J. Williams	X	8	8	8	8	8	X	40	12	480	120	15	17		152	520	
" " (overtime)	X	X	X	X	4	4	X	8	24	192							
K. Pudleigh	X	8	4	4	4	4	X	24	10	240	32	5	7		44	196	
F. Knight	X	8	8	X	8	8	8	40	10	400	76	9	12	16	113	287	
										2152	370	48	61	16	495	1657	

Do whatever is most convenient. The important thing is to have correct figures written down in the payroll book.

The accounting entries (if you are writing up the synoptic journal yourself) are not difficult.

If you pay net wages out of the till, your cash sheet summary or cash book column total will be a debit consisting of the total you have paid out. By putting through an entry like this (John, again):

Dr. Wages expense	$400.00	
Cr. Employee tax deductions		$ 75.00
Cr. Canada Pension Plan		6.00
Cr. Union dues		3.00
Cr. Savings bond		10.00
Cr. Unemployment insurance		9.00
Cr. Cash advances		20.00
Cr. Hospital insurance premium		4.00
Cr. Net wages due		273.00

you set up a credit which will exactly equal the amount you paid out of the till.

If you pay wages by individual cheque, the entries are the same except that the credit for $273.00 goes in the "Cr. Bank" column, rather than "Net Wages Due" (or perhaps General Ledger) column.

You can, if you wish, use the payroll book itself as a journal, or alternatively, you can write out the entry across the synoptic. Either way the figures will end up in the proper general ledger accounts.

The above example deals with John only. If you have a number of employees, for accounting purposes it is the payroll column *totals* that concern you, and not the individual amounts that make it up.

If you decide to use the payroll book as a journal, remember when you come to reconcile the bank at the month-end that not all your cheques are listed in the synoptic. The pay-cheques are in the payroll journal, and that is where you will have to tick them off to get your outstanding cheque list.

If you pay by cheque, date your cheques as if they were issued on payday, even if they are in fact issued a day or two later. This makes for an easier tie-in with the payroll book. And, incidentally, it is a good idea to put the cheque numbers opposite the amounts in the payroll book.

Avoid, if you possibly can, paying your employees in dribbles and drabbles. John has $273.00 coming to him. If he gets it in the form of cheques for $25.00, $30.00, $50.00, and $168.00, you are making work for yourself or your accountant, let alone incurring bank charges.

Sometimes you may employ somebody with the understanding that he or she will receive, say, $300 net per week, and that you will look after all income tax and other deductions.

When this happens you have to work backwards on the payroll sheet. Put down the net take-home pay first, then add back the tax to get gross pay earned. This may require a bit of juggling because when you add the tax you automatically jump your employee's wages and thus increase the tax deduction. This will work itself out if you experiment with various figures in the tax table.

Watch your deadlines for remitting income tax and pension plan deductions and unemployment insurance. If you are late, you may get governmental forgiveness once, but after that you can count on a penalty.

Occasionally, and to your annoyance, you will find you have made a mistake in subtracting the total deductions from an employee's gross wages. This usually happens when you issued the pay-cheques in a hurry and didn't stop to cross-balance the column totals at the time. When you do, you find you are 10 cents out, and on checking back over the individual lines, you find you underpaid John by that amount.

The easiest way to fix it is to cut John's gross pay for that week by 10 cents, and reduce the gross pay column accordingly. Then you can give John a 10-cent boost next week to square things. In fact, to adjust any error in your payroll arithmetic, leave the net pay as it stands and work back to an adjusted gross pay.

Whatever you do, don't leave the wrong figures sitting there. If you make up the payroll then you must cross-balance it.

In addition to keeping a payroll book, you (or your accountant) will need a running record of total pay and total income tax and pension contribution deducted for each employee. This can be kept on cards, ledger sheets, or in a scribbler, as long as the figures are right. And here, for your own protection, you should use the principle of the control account.

Your wages expense in the general ledger should always equal the total of all the "earnings to date" on employees' individual wage cards or sheets. And your total tax and pension deductions in the general ledger (all the credits in those two accounts) should likewise equal the total of all the tax and pension deductions to date on your employees' individual cards.

If you make sure these two items are correct, month by month, then you won't have to hunt for differences when John says "Hey, what's the idea? My wife kept all my pay slips and she says I didn't earn this much!"

12

INVENTORIES

Inventory is pronounced with the accent on the first syllable, not on the second. It means the goods you have to sell. They may be paid for, or not paid for, insured or not insured, new or second-hand — so long as you own them and acquired them with the idea of selling them at a profit, they are inventory. If you had to pay freight and cartage to get goods to where you can sell them, then freight and cartage are part of the cost of your inventory too.

Inventory is *not* any of the following:

(a) Furniture, fixtures, equipment, automobiles, land, buildings, machinery — anything that is a permanent part of your business and not normally offered for sale

(b) Goods left with you on consignment and still unsold. They are part of the inventory of the person who left them and who still owns them, but they are not part of your inventory

(c) Goods that have been sold and invoiced by you, but which have not yet been delivered to your customer

(d) Goods you have ordered, which may have been delivered to you, but which have not been invoiced to you yet

If you include any of the above four things in your inventory you will be deluding yourself into showing a profit you haven't got, and, more important, paying income tax you don't owe.

Parts (c) and (d) are, of course, primarily a matter of invoice cutoff dates. If you are taking inventory as at December 31, watch your invoice dates. For your own sales, don't make out any invoices until the goods have been actually shipped. For incoming stuff, look over suppliers' invoice dates in the first week of January, and if any of the goods are on your inventory sheets, strike them off.

One of the most sensible rules in accounting is that inventories should be valued at cost or market, whichever is the lower. You can take this absolutely literally. If you have obsolete stock, flyblown merchandise, damaged goods — in short, anything on which you know you are going to take a loss — list it at what you would pay for it if you were buying it "as is." If this means zero, make it zero. But be reasonable. Don't knock off 40% on general principles or just to be conservative. Understating your inventory means that when you do sell the stuff it will increase your income with a jump, perhaps into an unnecessarily higher income tax bracket.

Taking inventory is usually a long, wearisome business, and by the time you have counted everything and written it down (printed inventory sheets will save time) the thought of looking through a sheaf of supplier's invoices to find cost prices appalls you. You are inclined to say the heck with it, let's make an estimate.

As an accountant, as well as in the interests of accuracy, I would say, grit your teeth and stick to it, even if it does take five or six evenings working at home.

Moreover, the law of the land prescribes that you take inventory properly and have the sheets available for inspection if they are asked for by the tax department.

a. SHORT CUTS

There are, however, certain short cuts you may honorably take to reduce the arithmetic.

— You may cut out the pennies in your extension column, figuring to the nearest dollar, up or down. Your overs will roughly cancel out your shorts, so that the error in your final totals will be insignificant.

— You can adopt the same system when figuring prices per dozen — alter the price to the nearest dime, up or down.

— Don't bother weighing bulk goods to the nearest pound. You should be sufficiently familiar with your stock to tell at a glance within 10 pounds how much is in a barrel or sack. Again, your overs and shorts will come close to cancelling each other out.

— Abbreviate your descriptions as much as you can. You are the only person who has to interpret them.

— Total each inventory sheet separately and carry the totals to a summary sheet. This cuts out carrying forward a figure from one sheet to another, and thereby reduces the chances of error.

However, despite your good intentions, despite the pleas of your accountant and the tax department, let us suppose there comes a time when you have to make an estimate. You were at a party on December 31, and for a week after New Year's Day you are laid up with a heavy head cold. Comes January 6 and no inventory taken. What to do?

The best thing would be to take inventory as of the sixth, add back your estimate of the cost of the goods sold within the last six days and take off the cost of goods purchased in that time. The way you will come very close to your December 31 figure.

However, suppose that is not feasible. What then?

Well, what we're going to do is not good accounting, but at least it will give you a figure to work with. It is in two steps.

STEP 1

Put down your sales figure for the year.
Suppose it is $50 000.00
Now figure the percentage of profit in your
average sales dollar. Suppose it is 20%. Then,
to make a profit of 20% of $50 000.00, that is 10 000.00
you must have sold goods that cost you $40 000.00

STEP 2

You know your opening inventory was $ 2 500.00
and you know from your records that you
bought goods during the year costing 42 000.00
making a total of 44 500.00
therefore, to make the cost of goods sold
what you think it was, you should have a
closing inventory of 4 500.00
which would make the *net* cost of goods
sold the way you figured it, viz. $40 000.00

In actual practice your estimated inventory would not work out to a round figure such as $4 500, which is just as well. Because if you put down $4 500 for your closing inventory, it would look like the simon-pure estimate it is, and the tax assessor might ask to see your inventory sheets, which could be rather embarrassing.

Step 2 represents the oldest formula in bookkeeping, the one by which you figure out the cost of goods sold during a fiscal period. Normally, of course, you *know* your closing inventory and you don't know the cost of goods sold.

Sometimes the formula is arranged in a slightly different way, thus:

Purchases during the year $42 000.00
Less — Inventory adjustment:
   opening $ 2 500.00
   closing 4 500.00 2 000.00
Cost of goods sold $40 000.00

144

The net result is the same. If your inventory has decreased, then it is "plus" inventory adjustment, rather than "less."

The correctness of your profit figure is dependent on the accuracy of your inventory, no more, no less. If you overestimate your closing inventory by $100, your profit for the year will be overstated by that amount, and vice versa.

The variations you may encounter and the results they will produce can be summarized in a table.

Opening Inventories	Closing Inventories	Profits
Correct	Over	Overstated
Correct	Under	Understated
Over	Correct	Understated
Under	Correct	Overstated
Over	Over (same amount)	Correct
Under	Under (same amount)	Correct

b. OVER- OR UNDER-STATING

Most people lean toward underestimating their closing inventories, a tendency which becomes pronounced around income tax time. Leaners should keep in mind, though, that they are only putting off the evil day. If you kept lowering your inventory every year, there would come a time when you hit bottom, and from then on you would have to report a profit which, politely speaking, was more realistic.

Furthermore, there may come a day when you decide to sell your business, and the buyer insists on a correct inventory valuation in the bill of sale. Your income for that final year will positively bulge with the cumulative amounts you have knocked down in previous years.

And yet another point you should keep in mind: all similar businesses tend to show a similar gross profit percentage and this fact is well known to the tax department. If you consistently show a smaller percentage than other people in the same business, you will receive a visitor with a briefcase under his or her arm who would like to know why your business is different.

The moral of all this seems to be, "when valuing your inventory, be conservative, but don't be greedy."

Sometimes you may have heard someone mention "perpetual inventory," and you wondered what it meant.

A perpetual inventory is a running stock-record. Usually it is kept on cards, one item to a card, with "in," "out," and "balance" columns, like a ledger page.

A perpetual inventory is not practical in the average retail store because the amount of detail would swamp whomever tried to run it. It requires written records, either delivery order, invoice, or a combination of both, from which to enter "out" figures. The "in" figures can be obtained from suppliers' invoices or your own purchase orders as goods are checked into stock.

It is used extensively by parts supply houses, and with good reason. With thousands of parts to sell, and each part of supreme importance to the man who wants it in a hurry, the parts dealer must know promptly when he needs to reorder. He can get this information more easily from stock ledger cards than from ambulating around the parts bin every night and deciding which items look low.

You can use a perpetual inventory in your business if the information it yields is worth the trouble of maintaining the system. It may even pay you to maintain stock cards for selected important items. But whether your inventory is carried on cards or you have graduated to a computer print-out, stock ledger clerks can make mistakes, and sales clerks have been known to feed absolute nonsense into a machine, so it is still necessary to take a physical count from time to time.

You will enjoy one advantage, however, with a perpetual inventory. You don't have to take stock on the last day of your fiscal year. You can do it when convenient, one section at a time, throughout the year. Then, at your year-end when you list your inventory from your stock cards, you can do it with confidence, for you will know that every item in the list will have been checked by actual count at least once a year.

c. WORK IN PROGRESS

If you are in the manufacturing business, whether it be canned goods, truck bodies, houses, or anything else, you are going to encounter an inventory problem which your more fortunate fellow-taxpayers escape. It will be up to you to set a value on partly completed work.

There are no rules for this, other than the application of common sense.

You should be sufficiently close to your business to have a reasonable idea of what your work-in-progress has cost you to date. It is not likely that anyone will argue over the figure you decide on, and, in your case, if you decide on $5 000.00, round figure or not, the tax department will likely accept it.

Even you, however, cannot escape from the effect of underestimating or overestimating on subsequent years' profits. When you have sold your last case of canned goods, your last truck body or your last bungalow, the rightness or wrongness of your previous inventory estimates will finally float to the surface.

d. SPECIAL CASES

Let's assume you are in the business of selling large, high-priced items, such as recreational vehicles (RVs), grand pianos, farm equipment, or any enterprise where the number of units sold is low but the price per unit is high.

If you operate one of these, you shouldn't try to get by with dumping everything into a Purchases account and relying on an inventory figure taken every so often for an interim or year-end statement. What you need is a "Current Inventory" system.

Whether it is on a tray of cards, a loose-leaf binder, or whatever, this involves entering the cost of every unit in your inventory on its own page in a subsidiary ledger and keeping the dollar total of all the pages in balance with an "Inventory Control" account in the general ledger.

You are dealing with large amounts of money and you can't afford anything less than tight inventory control. With relatively fewer sales the paperwork is not onerous.

We will assume you have an RV franchise and you have just taken delivery of three new units on your lot. In practice this would result in an entry across the columns in a journal entry page, but for convenience let's put it in journal entry form, thus:

Dr. Vehicle Inventory	$65 000.00	
Cr. Accounts Payable		$65 000.00

To record delivery of our Purchase order No. 101, from XL Mfg. Co. Inc. as follows:

1 Model A Motorhome, Stock No. xx,	$23 000.00
1 Model B Motorhome, Stock No. xx,	27 000.00
1 Model Y Travel Trailer, Stock No. xx,	15 000.00

The next part of a Current Inventory system requires a "Dr. Cost of Sales" column in the sales journal, with a corresponding account in the general ledger. To illustrate, let's say you have just sold a 20-foot trailer for $14 000. The entry in the sales journal, disregarding minor details such as sales tax, customer's name, stock number, etc., would be as follows:

Dr. Cash	$14 000.00	
Cr. Sales		$14 000.00
Dr. Cost of Sales	$11 000.00	
Cr. Vehicle Inventory		$11 000.00

except that once again it would be spread across the page on one line or a group of lines.

The first two lines in the above entry are old friends from your sales journal, but the next two accomplish something new. They tell you at a glance your gross profit on the sale, and at the same time you know your inventory has been "relieved" of a unit that is no longer in stock.

At your month-end the Cr. Sales and Dr. Cost of Sales column totals will provide you with an exact gross profit figure for the month, and the Cr. Vehicle Inventory column tells you precisely how much your inventory has been reduced by sales.

Often a unit purchased will require extra parts, optional equipment, mechanical work, or other alterations to make it more saleable. Debit your inventory card (and the control account) with the amount expended so that you will have an accurate figure for the Cost of Goods Sold column when the unit is sold. The credit side of the above entry would go into an expense account or to your regular Purchases account, where all your "non-unit" but otherwise saleable merchandise is charged.

To sum up, all your journals are exactly the same as the ones you have become used to *except* —

(a) in your purchase journal units are debited in the Dr. Vehicle Inventory column, and

(b) in your sales journal each sales entry is accompanied by —

　(i)　a debit in the Cost of Sales column, and

　(ii)　an identical credit in the Cr. Vehicle Inventory column.

All of the above are on the same line or group of lines in the journal.

149

The "Current Inventory" concept outlined above can be profitably applied in many enterprises such as subdivision, housing, general contracting, major equipment manufacturing, and, in short, any place where the amount of each sale is large and the applicable cost can be readily isolated. Basically it is an elementary form of cost accounting. Don't venture too far afield without it.

13

THE BALANCE SHEET

A balance sheet is a combination of three things —

> — a list of what you own,
> — a list of what you owe, and
> — the difference between the two.

The first list is commonly headed "Assets," the second list "Liabilities," and the difference is known by a number of names, including Capital, Proprietorship, Proprietary Equity, Share Issue, Proprietor's Investment, and Net Worth. Of all these I personally prefer Net Worth. It fits the facts and has the force of brevity, but for some reason it seems to be used least.

At any rate, the net worth of your business is what you would receive if all your assets were sold at book value, the proceeds used to pay off your debts, and the remainder handed to you in the form of a cheque.

The most sensible way to show your net worth would be like this:

Assets	$500.00
Less: Liabilities	300.00
Net Worth	$200.00

but, except in a few ignorant countries where they don't know any better, you hardly ever run across the sensible way. Instead, you will find balance sheets shown like this:

Assets	$500.00	Liabilities	$300.00
		Net Worth	200.00
		Total	$500.00

This arrangement is favored because accountants feel a warm, comfortable glow whenever they see two equal totals side by side.

Accountants, I regret to say, have condoned the bad habit of heading the right-hand side of the balance sheet "Liabilities" instead of "Liabilities and Net Worth." This confuses a lot of businesspeople no end because they have always understood that a liability means money owed, and their natural reaction is "That's ridiculous! I don't owe my net worth to anyone!"

At about this point the accountant steps in and insists that the business owes that to them (the businesspeople).

This makes the whole picture as clear as mud and, anyway, nobody can understand the way accountants think, so the balance sheet is put to one side and the income statement brought out, where at least an expense is an expense because the cheques most definitely went through the bank.

The best plan, therefore, is to remember that the right-hand side of the balance sheet *should* be headed "Liabilities and Net Worth," but frequently isn't.

Many balance sheets are written out like this:

Assets	$500.00
Liabilities	$300.00
Net Worth	200.00
Total	$500.00

This is called a balance sheet in "statement form" (as against "account form") adhered to by many accountants because it doesn't require a wide-carriage typewriter. Fortunately it is also easier to read, as the eye follows vertical figures more easily than horizontal ones.

Now that you've met the basic principle behind the balance sheet, let's have a look at the details with which it is customarily fluffed out.

Don't think these details are unimportant. They give perspective, the same way that light and shadows give depth to a picture. They show whether your money is liquid or frozen and, if the latter, how much energy is needed to thaw it out. They show whether your creditors can jump on you with both feet or merely kick you if you don't meet debt instalments.

But despite the voluminous and detailed information that may appear on a balance sheet, you should never forget this maxim:

A BALANCE SHEET IS ONLY AS GOOD AS THE FACTS BEHIND THE FIGURES.

Accounts receivable may contain disputed accounts, inventories may be full of obsolete goods, and equipment may be worth very much less than the book values shown. Liabilities may have been "forgotten," and disputed income tax assessments may hang heavily in the air — but not on the balance sheet.

On the reverse side of the coin (particularly if it is an old established business), there may be assets carried on the books at only a fraction of what they are really worth.

Equipment, for instance, is often written off at the rate of 10% of cost each year, and yet some 10-year-old equipment may still have a long period of useful life ahead of it.

Many of these things, pro and con, can be smelled out by a smart auditor, but even the smartest won't guarantee that the final figure for the net worth of the business is exactly what it should be.

Auditors guarantee nothing. They will say that the figures are "according to the books," and that "in their opinion" they are correct. And they will say that only after they have made a thorough search for evidence that would indicate otherwise.

So the next time you hear anybody say that his or her books have been audited and the balance sheet is correct to the penny, you will know that so far as the books go, that is probably right. But so far as the values go, it means that an auditor has approved what he or she considered to be an intelligent estimate.

a. CONTENTS OF A BALANCE SHEET

Now turn to the sample balance sheet, Sample #22, and we'll go over the headings and titles, one by one.

CURRENT ASSETS: Sometimes called "Quick Assets" because, in theory, they can be turned into cash without delay, i.e., in the course of current operations.

CASH: In a small business cash on hand is often shown separately from cash in the bank. In larger businesses they are combined.

ACCOUNTS RECEIVABLE: All the money owed to you, principally trade accounts. If you have any non-trade receivables they should be shown under a subheading, like this:

Accounts Receivable:	
Trade	$5 000.00
Loan	1 000.00
Tax Refundable	400.00
	$6 400.00

RESERVE FOR BAD DEBTS: Your estimate of the uncollectible accounts still on the books. Without this you would be fooling yourself, let alone other people who might examine your balance sheet.

INVENTORY OF MERCHANDISE: At cost price or market price, whichever is the lower.

SAMPLE #22
BALANCE SHEET

ASSETS

CURRENT ASSETS:

Cash on hand		$ 200.00	
Cash in Bank		1 593.00	
Accounts Receivable	$ 4 381.00		
Less: Reserve for Bad Debts	650.00	3 731.00	
Merchandise Inventory		6 469.00	
Utility Deposits		75.00	$ 12 068.00

FIXED ASSETS:

Building — at cost	24 000.00		
Less: Reserve for Depreciation	3 600.00	20 400.00	
Truck — at cost	1 200.00		
Less: Reserve for Depreciation	300.00	900.00	
Furniture & Fixtures — at cost	975.00		
Less: Reserve for Depreciation	292.00	683.00	
Land		5 000.00	26 983.00

DEFERRED CHARGES:

Prepaid Insurance	258.00

GOODWILL:

	500.00
	$ 39 809.00

LIABILITIES & CAPITAL

CURRENT LIABILITIES:

Bank Loan	$1 500.00	
Accounts Payable — Trade	2 235.00	
Sundry Creditors	327.00	
Sales Taxes Payable	98.00	$4 160.00

MORTGAGE:

	1 750.00

CAPITAL:

J. Spiff, Investment as at Dec. 31, 19—	32 048.00	
Add: Profit for the year	9 851.00	
	41 899.00	
Deduct: Drawings	8 000.00	
J. Spiff, Investment as at Dec. 31, 19—		33 899.00
		$ 39 809.00

UTILITIES DEPOSITS: The gas company or the power company insists on these. A small business carries them on the balance sheet so they won't be overlooked.

FIXED ASSETS: The permanent equipment used in your business, not ordinarily for resale. Fixed assets are usually shown in groups, such as buildings, machinery, automobiles, etc., for the reason that each group has a different rate of write-off.

RESERVES FOR DEPRECIATION: See chapter 8 on depreciation.

DEFERRED CHARGES: Sometimes called "Prepaid Expenses." Both titles are correct. A deferred charge is the unused portion of an expense you have to pay in advance, such as insurance, property taxes, workers' compensation, etc. Most of these things have a cash value of sorts, and for that reason they are often shown under the "Current Assets" grouping. However, the cash values are open to question, and, in fact, if you ever go broke, they are likely to evaporate.

GOODWILL: This was discussed fully in "On Buying a Business." It is not considered good accounting to show goodwill unless it has been actually paid for. In fact, many large corporations make a practice of writing down goodwill to $1 and displaying it prominently on the balance sheet at that figure. This is supposed to show shareholders that the management is conservative, in the good old-fashioned sense. (Alternatively, it may mean that goodwill is worth $1.)

CURRENT LIABILITIES: So called because they will have to be paid in the near future, i.e., in the course of "current" operations, usually considered as the next 12 months.

BANK OVERDRAFT: Not shown on the sample balance sheet because ordinarily you don't have money in the bank and an overdraft at the same time. If you are enjoying an overdraft this is where it appears.

BANK LOAN: This is in the current liabilities group because most bank loans have to be paid off, or at least whittled down, in less than 12 months.

ACCOUNTS PAYABLE: Nearly always confined to trade accounts for goods and services, but can include everything you owe. The non-trade accounts, such as employee tax deductions, trust funds on hand, unemployment insurance owed, and, in general, anything owed to any government department or bureau, should be listed separately from your trade payables. These creditors have preference if you go broke, and hence, by looking at your balance sheet, your other creditors should be able to tell what crumbs will be left for them.

FIXED LIABILITIES: On the balance sheet of a big company this is where you would find 20-year 9% bonds listed. It's not likely you enjoy such luxuries, but you may have a mortgage, or some other debt that doesn't have to be paid all at once.

If you buy a truck and the instalment payments have more than a year to run, your accountant might list the unpaid balance under a subheading, such as "Truck Notes Payable," in this section.

According to orthodox accounting theory, every debt due within 12 months should be in current liabilities. However, this rule should be modified according to circumstances. The year over which a small store may spread payments for a truck may be more important to the proprietor than the 20 years in which a large corporation can build up a sinking fund for bond redemption.

CAPITAL (OR NET WORTH): Your stake in the business. Often you will see it arranged on the balance sheet like this:

J. Spiff,

Investment in business Jan. 1/19-	$10 000.00
Add: Profit for the year ended Dec. 31/19-	9 000.00
	$19 000.00
Less: Drawings	8 000.00
J. Spiff,	
Investments as at Dec. 31/19-	<u>$11 000.00</u>

which tells the story with no words wasted.

If you are looking at the balance sheet of a corporation, you will find the arrangement a little different. This is because a corporation must always show the amount of the shareholders' original investment, plus a separate account called "Earned Surplus" or "Retained Earnings," in which are shown any profits that have been retained in the business by the management and not paid out as dividends. Hence the Capital group of accounts will look like this:

CAPITAL:

Authorized: 1 000 shares at $100 per share	<u>$100 000.00</u>
Issued and Fully paid:	
500 shares at $100 per share	50 000.00
EARNED SURPLUS,	
as at Dec. 31/19-	11 232.00
	<u>$61 232.00</u>

Earned Surplus has a little statement all of its own, tucked away at the bottom of the page, or even on a separate page. It will look like this:

Earned Surplus, as at Jan. 1/19-		$ 8 491.00
Profits for the year ended Dec. 31/19-		12 741.00
		$21 232.00
Less:		
Dividend No. 72, Aug. 15/19-	$5 000.00	
Transferred to Reserve for Taxes	5 000.00	10 000.00
Earned Surplus, as at Dec./19-		<u>$11 232.00</u>

158

This is exactly the same kind of information that appears on your own balance sheet, except that it is in corporation language.

"Surplus" is another of those accounting terms which cause confusion in the ranks of non-accountants. The accountant's surplus is different from the dictionary surplus. It's like the accountant's reserve for depreciation, in that neither of them mean money in the bank waiting to be used.

What surplus *does* mean is this: book profits left after dividends and taxes, and *not necessarily* left in the form of cash.

It is like the profit figure shown at the bottom of your income statement. You may have made $10 000 according to the books, but, if you had started from scratch, all that profit might be locked up in new equipment, inventory, and outstanding charge accounts. You made it, to be sure, but you've ploughed it back into the business.

That's why a corporation may have half a million dollars in its earned surplus account and still have to borrow money from the bank to meet its payroll.

Sometimes a business loses money continuously, so that not only does the original investment disappear, but the business exists only by the grace of God and its creditors. Instead of a surplus there is a deficit.

On our original balance sheet the situation would be presented thus:

ASSETS		LIABILITIES	
Assets		Liabilities	
(detailed list)	$300.00	(detailed list)	$500.00
		Less: Deficit	200.00
			$300.00

Sometimes, I regret to say, it will be presented thus:

ASSETS		LIABILITIES
Assets		
(detailed list)	$300.00	
Deficit	200.00	Liabilities
	$500.00	(detailed list) $500.00

The above arrangement should be banned in all civilized countries on the grounds that to call a deficit an asset is against public morals. However, there will always be some accountants who dislike subtraction, so don't be surprised if you encounter it.

There are other titles and subtitles you will find on balance sheets, especially those published by large corporations. However, if you analyze the figures you will find that, stripped of double-talk, they all boil down to the basic equation:

Assets = Liabilities + Net Worth

b. INCOME STATEMENTS

Your balance sheet is important, but your income statement is more so. Your balance sheet tells you how you stood on such and such a day, but your income statement (or income summary, income sheet, profit and loss statement) tells you how you got there, and from it you may reasonably surmise where you are going.

It is much easier to understand than a balance sheet. The revenue figure sits at the top, and beneath it all the expenses cascade down the page to an expense total. The difference between revenue and expense is profit.

But let's deal with the figures as they appear because even an income statement may contain variations from standard.

REVENUE — nearly always sales, but could be interest, dividends, fees or any other source of income, *provided* the main body of expenses were incurred in the course of earning it. On the statement of a large concern you may find a *gross* sales figure, from which sales returns and allowances are deducted, to give a *net* sales figure.

COST OF GOODS SOLD — The time-honored formula explained in the inventories chapter comes in here. In addition to purchases you will often find cartage and freight included in this section, and also wages if they are directly related to the goods sold.

GROSS PROFIT — or gross trading profit. If you had no overhead expenses this would be all yours.

The principal use of this figure is to determine whether or not you are getting a big enough spread between cost and selling price.

The gross profit percentage is obtained by dividing your sales figure into your gross profits figure. Thus on the first income statement illustrated (see Sample #23) the gross profit percentage is:

$$\frac{25\ 522 \times 100}{102\ 910} = 24.8\%$$

EXPENSES — There is a whole chapter on the subject of individual expenses and little more can be said, except that sometimes you will find them grouped in classes instead of in a long string.

This is due to the way accountants are trained. When they are young it is firmly impressed on them that expenses should be broken down into the following:

— selling expenses
— general and administrative expenses
— financial expenses

and consequently when they draw up an income statement for anything bigger than a corner store, they instinctively follow this "examination paper" pattern. The second statement (see Sample #24) illustrates this treatment.

161

SALES DISCOUNTS (2% – 10 days) — This is sometimes shown as a deduction from gross sales (like sales returns), and sometimes as a financial expense. Fierce controversies have raged in accounting circles on where discounts should appear on the statement, and no doubt both sides are absolutely right.

The fact remains that whether you arrive at your net profit by putting expenses in groups or by one jump, the final result won't change.

The layout of an income statement should be such that it conveys a maximum of information to the person entitled to see it. If it conveys less, then the reader will surmise that you are trying to hide something.

Big corporation statements often convey a calculated minimum. This is because the directors fear that anything more would give away valuable information to competitors.

Some corporations do exactly the opposite. They publish detailed charts and diagrams, showing exactly how much money was taken in and where it was spent. This practice, however, is pretty well confined to corporations big enough to not give a hoot about competitors.

J. SPIFF & COMPANY
Income Statement For the Year Ended December 31, 19—

SALES		$102 910
COST OF SALES		
Opening Inventory	$ 7 306	
Add: Purchases	76 551	
	83 857	
Less: Closing Inventory	6 469	77 388
GROSS PROFIT		25 522
EXPENSES		
Accounting	600	
Advertising	328	
Bad debts	100	
Delivery	417	
Insurance	255	
Laundry	238	
Licenses & Permits	140	
Light & Power	456	
Miscellaneous	221	
Mortgage interest	226	
Payroll & other taxes	655	
Rent	960	
Repairs & Maintenance	683	
Stationery & stamps	142	
Supplies & wrapping paper	875	
Taxes	842	
Wages	6 936	

Depreciation			
— Building	$ 1 200		
— Truck	300		
— Furniture & fixtures	97	1 597	15 671

Net Profit, to Balance Sheet		$ 9 851

J. SPIFF & COMPANY LTD.
Income Statement For the Year Ended Dec. 31, 19—

REVENUE

Gross Sales		$205 000
Less: Sales Returns	$ 1 500	
Sales Discounts	2 000	3 500
Net Sales		201 500

COST OF GOODS SOLD

Inventory of Mdse: Dec. 31,19—	25 000	
Add: Purchases	150 000	
Freight Inwards	3 000	
	178 000	
Deduct: Inventory of Mdse. Dec. 31, 19—	23 000	155 000
TRADING PROFIT		46 500

SELLING EXPENSES

Advertising	3 000	
Delivery Costs	2 000	
Sales Commissions Paid	5 000	
Sales Salaries	15 000	25 000
SELLING PROFIT		21 500

GENERAL AND ADMINISTRATIVE EXPENSES

Donations	250	
Insurance	300	
Legal and Accounting	700	
Light, Power and Fuel	850	
Office and Stationery	1 290	
Rent	2 400	
Executive Salaries	10 000	
Telegraph and Telephone	762	16 552
OPERATING PROFIT		4 948

FINANCIAL EXPENSE

Bad Debts written off	2 500	
Interest Expense	200	
	2 700	
Less: Interest earned	230	2 470
NET PROFIT, transferred to Statement of Earned Surplus		$ 2 478

14

WHAT IS "CASH FLOW"?

This is an impressive-sounding phrase you will run into from time to time, mainly from people who want to lend you money.

Bank managers like the sound of it because it conjures up a vision of dollars streaming through your business and into the bank, where, naturally enough, some of them will be sidetracked for services rendered.

Keep in mind, though, that there will be times when money flows out of your business faster than it flows in, thereby causing that frequent headache called "shortage of working capital."

This is usually a seasonal situation: Christmas rush, spring fashions, vacation activities, or anything that reaches a foreseeable peak regularly each year and consequently has to be prepared for with adequate stock and perhaps extra personnel.

When the need arises, your accountant can readily make up a detailed projected cash flow statement to fit the picture. In effect, he writes up a brief imaginary set of books for a given future period, and then takes off a series of brief imaginary "Source and Application of Funds" statements to see how the cash position looks at different intervals.

These statements are either based on figures from previous years' experience, in which case you should have a pretty good idea of what they will indicate, or else pure conjecture, in which case try to restrain your inborn optimism.

However, no matter how many beautiful projections your accountant may turn out, the best way to avoid cash flow problems (e.g., shortage of cash) is to use ordinary common sense.

As the manager of your business, you are engaged in one transaction after another in buying and selling. If you sold for cash as fast as you could buy for cash, nothing would go wrong and profits would pile up.

But, you've got to tie up cash in inventory and/or accounts receivable (particularly in the seasonal situations mentioned above), and if you are buying assets on time payments you've got to tie up money in equipment. If you borrowed money to get started, you've got to work off loans.

The moral of all this is not to get out of your depth.

By all means get the longest terms you can manage from your trade suppliers, and certainly negotiate a revolving bank loan when necessary, but in the final analysis, unless you have rich relatives to turn to, the safe and steady growth of your business is going to depend on leaving the maximum possible amount of profit therein.

Have your accountant project a cash flow statement if it will make your bank happy — and then see how the estimate compares with what eventually happens.

This activity will take you well along toward "budgeting," which is another word bank managers like to hear when you apply for a loan.

Budgeting (or forecasting) means making reasonably intelligent guesses as to revenue and expenses for any given future period, and the logical layout for this business forecast is your income statement.

Dress up your statement with extra columns, showing forecast vs. actual figures, either monthly, quarterly, or annually, and fill in the actual sets of figures as they become available. The difference between the two sets of figures ("over" or "under" budget) deserves your careful attention, for they will immediately point up dangerously out-of-line expenses. The comparison will indicate whether your sales are up to expectations and whether your margin of profit on sales is what it should be.

Lack of profitable sales can't be rectified by bookkeeping procedures, but at least you will be aware of it, and can take steps to remedy the condition.

So keep an eye on the direction in which your revenue and expense totals are heading, and don't grumble if you find yourself lying awake at night figuring out how to make more and better sales.

That's the price you pay for independence.

15

THE GENERAL JOURNAL

Up to this point you have been coasting along in the general area of bookkeeping without, I hope, too many problems. If you have been writing up the journals yourself, you should now feel thoroughly at home with debits and credits and when your accountant arrives after the end of the month you no longer stand around in silent awe.

But, at this stage you have to make two decisions. Do you want to leave as much of the clerical work as possible to your accountant? Do you believe that revenue is far more important than bookwork? If you feel the answers to these questions are "yes," then you can safely skip the next three chapters and hurry back to making bigger and better sales.

If, on the other hand, you are consumed with curiosity about what happens next in the general ledger and how to take off financial statements, then this and the two following chapters will give you detailed information.

a. JOURNAL ENTRIES

The first step toward becoming a full-fledged bookkeeper is to learn how to tidy up a number of technical loose ends left around. This is done with journal entries.

On page 85 you will see a reference to the general journal. In the days before accounting machines and computers, this was a frightfully important-looking volume with the title imprinted on the cover in large gold letters. It was so important that it was entrusted exclusively to the care of an elderly head bookkeeper who was the only person authorized to make general journal entries.

You don't have to impress a roomful of clerks, but I suggest you get a proper two-column book instead of trying to squeeze the general journal into the back pages of the synoptic.

As to journal entries, they will never give you any trouble as long as you remember two essential points:

(a) There may be one or more debits and one or more credits making up the entry, but the totals of the debits and credits must be equal.

(b) When you have written in your figures always put in a "narrative," which is the accounting term for a brief explanation beneath the entry. If you don't do this you may have a hard time a year from now remembering what the entry was all about, and if you ever had an auditor looking over your books he or she will definitely have a harder time.

The journal entries you will be making can be divided roughly into two classes:

(a) Entries made once a month, being the bare minimum needed to keep your records up to date.

(b) Entries required only when you take off a financial statement, either monthly, quarterly, semi-annually, or at the end of your fiscal year.

Of course there are other times when a journal entry is needed, such as when you have to correct a mistake. (An accountant never makes a mistake. If he has done something wrong, and after a discreet interval, he will "make the necessary adjustment.") But by and large your journal entries will fall into two basic categories.

b. MONTHLY ENTRIES

If you have anybody working for you, right away you are going to run into a minor complication arising from the Canada Pension Plan (CPP) and Unemployment Insurance (UIC).

This is because your remittance to the government is a combination of employee deductions and an additional amount representing your contribution, which is an expense.

When you entered the figures from the payroll in Sample #21, you posted a credit of $40 to the UIC account in the general ledger. This represents the amount deducted from your employees' wages for the week and so far, so good.

Let's say there are four pay periods in the month and for easy figuring the other three weeks are also $40, making a total of $160 in credits for January, 19-.

Before the February deadline you have to send in to the government the above $160, *plus* $160 multiplied by 1.4, which is $224, making a grand total of $384 for the cheque.

When you write up the general ledger, you will have in the UIC account the $160 credit from the payroll and the $384.00 debit from the cheque (both posted from a journal, of course), leaving a debit balance of $224, which is your UIC expense for the month. Very informative, you say, but unfortunately it is also bad bookkeeping.

It's bad because you're mixing up a liability and an expense in one account. There is a far better way to handle the situation, and it is very simple.

You should have two UIC accounts — one for the liability and the other for the expense.

The $160 obtained from your employees is definitely a liability because you owe it to the government. It is also a part of the bottom line of the payroll journal totals which are neatly cross-balanced and cannot be tinkered with. So you

170

decide to make the existing UIC ledger page the liability account.

But the $224 balance (after you have posted the cheque) is an expense — so you write out an entry in the general journal to transfer it into a properly labelled account, like this:

Dr. UIC expense $224.00

    Cr. UIC liability $224.00

to record employer's contribution for the month of January, 19-

When you post the above figures you will, quite properly, reduce the balance in the liability account to zero. On the other hand you will have established an account in which will accumulate, month by month, your total UIC expense for the year.

Normally, you will clear out the liability account each month with a cheque. If you don't sent it in or if you are late, the liability remains on the books, which is as it should be. If you accidentally send in too much or too little, it's easy to look back and see what happened. In either event you no longer have a mixture which is neither an expense nor a liability.

The same procedure applies to your CPP figures. There should be one account for the liability and a second for the expense. The layout of the journal entry is along the same lines as that for the UIC.

For employees' tax deductions there are no complications because you don't have to contribute any amount yourself. No expense is involved so all you need is an in-and-out liability account.

The next monthly entry that can conveniently go in the general journal is your cash analysis (if you have one).

If you look back at the synoptic journals in Samples #16 and #18, you can't help noticing how lopsided the column of debits looks in the general ledger column against the vast area of white paper on the rest of the page. The general journal with its two-only columns eliminates this depressing waste of space.

If you are *not* posting from your payroll journal directly to the general ledger, more space can be saved if you put your payroll totals in the general journal either weekly or as totals for the month. In fact you should always use the general journal if, by doing so, you can avoid filling up the synoptic with bits and pieces.

c. PERIODIC ENTRIES

There are a number of periodic entries and although some of them may not apply to your business, it's a good idea to list them, with an explanation in case you have to decide whether you need the entry of not.

1. Sales tax commission

If you collect sales tax at the retail level, very often a considerate government will let you keep a small percentage of the tax, ostensibly to cover the expenses of collection. This will require a journal entry, as under:

Dr. Sales tax payable $30.00

    Cr. Sundry commission revenue $30.00
to record sales tax commission for the month of January, 19-

The above assumes you collected $1 000.00 in tax during the month and that the taxing authority allows you 3% commission. The $30 debit when posted to the general ledger will reduce the Sales Tax payable account from $1 000 to $970, which in turn will be reduced to zero when you post the cheque paying the balance. The credit entries will build up, month by month, until you have a cumulative commission total for the year.

I don't want to confuse you, but if you want to save a line of writing there is an alternative way to pick up the commission. When you enter the $970 cheque in the synoptic and spread the balancing figures across the page, they would be:

172

Dr. Sales tax payable $1 000.00
    Cr. Sundry commission revenue $ 30.00
    Cr. Bank   970.00

This eliminates the monthly journal entry. However, it is inaccurate in that it only recognizes the $30 commission when you pay the tax and not when you earned it, which is usually a month earlier.

All of the above refers to provincial sales taxes only, as there is definitely no commission allowed for collecting the GST.

2. Prepaid insurance

Almost every business carries insurance of one kind or another, for which the premiums are customarily paid when the policy is issued. Let's assume you are taking off a statement at the end of your fiscal year, in which case this is the entry you will need:

Dr. Insurance expense $185.00
    Cr. Prepaid insurance $185.00
to record insurance expired during the five months ended December 31, 19-

This shows that in August you paid a $445 premium for a one-year policy, at which time you debited the entire amount to Prepaid Insurance (or Deferred Charges) in the general ledger. By the end of December you've used up $5/12$ths of the insurance, so the prepaid part is reduced proportionately.

3. Mortgage interest

If your building or any other substantial asset used in your business is encumbered with a mortgage, then interest is accruing continuously. To find out how much has accrued during the year you will have to refer to your computer printout and add up the 12 monthly figures in the interest column. Then you can make an adjusting entry, as follows:

Dr. Interest expense $2 196.20
    Cr. Mortgage payable $2 196.20
to adjust for mortgage interest as at December 31, 19-

The reason you had to make a 12-month adjustment is because you always seemed to be in a hurry when you entered the monthly principal-and-interest cheques of $400, so each time you debited the Mortgage Payable account with the full amount of the cheque. If you had *not* been in a hurry you would have entered a typical payment like this:

Dr. Interest expense $176.29
Dr. Mortgage payable $223.71
     Cr. Bank $400.00

to record mortgage payment of the month of June, 19-, as per computer printout

except that it wouldn't have been a general journal entry but on a regular line in the synoptic in sequence with your other cheques for the month.

4. Depreciation

Normally depreciation is calculated and entered once a year. You can do it on a monthly basis if you wish, but that tends to use up a lot of lines in the general ledger. (If you really need a monthly figure it *is* possible to do it without cluttering up the books, as you will see in chapter 17.)

The regular depreciation entries are simple and self-explanatory.

Dr. Depreciation expense, building   xxxx
     Cr. Reserve for depreciation, building   xxxx
to write off building at the rate of 5% per annum for the year 19-

The same treatment is accorded any other depreciable assets on your books.

5. Accrued wages

If you pay your employees every two weeks and the last pay period ends after the end of the month, your wages expense will be incorrect on a monthly income statement. Even on a year-end statement if you don't show accrued and unpaid wages it can result in up to a 4% error in your wages total for the year. The necessary adjusting entry is straightforward:

Dr. Wages expense   xxxx
      Cr. Accrued wages   xxxx

to set up liability for gross wages owed but unpaid for the last eight days of 19-

In a small business the accrued CPP and UIC expense is not significant, but setting up gross unpaid wages is a must.

Once you are into the new year this entry should be reversed, thus:

Dr. Accrued wages (sundry creditors)   xxxx
      Cr. Wages expense   xxxx

to reverse accrual set up for the last eight days of 19-

Without this entry, your new year's wages total will remain with eight days too much in it.

6. Interest revenue

Sometimes you find yourself on the receiving end of a mortgage or other long-term indebtedness, in which case interest is accruing continuously in your favor.

You can pick this up with the following entry:

Dr. Interest receivable   xxxx
      Cr. Interest revenue   xxxx

to record interest accrued on mortgage for January, 19-

If you have a printed notice on your invoices or statements to the effect that interest on overdue accounts will be charged at a certain percent per month, you can make an entry once a month like this:

Dr. Accounts receivable   xxx
Company A   xxx
Company B   xxx
Company C   xxx
                        <u>xxxx</u>
      Cr. Interest revenue   xxxx

to record interest on overdue accounts for the month of January, 19-

Frankly when an account reaches the point where you are charging overdue interest every month the odds are that the debtor firm will be full of excuses as to why they are late and why they will not pay the interest, and the account is teetering on the edge of bad debt status and you're not going to see much of your money, let alone the interest.

An alternative is to add interest to the monthly statement when it's sent out, and if it is eventually paid, credit it in the synoptic in the general ledger column. If it happens all the time, start a credit column headed "Overdue Interest Collected."

7. Bad debts

Every business that gives credit will eventually incur some doubtful or bad debts and, from an accounting point of view, this leads to a rather interesting situation. If you want to impress your bank manager with a substantial-looking balance sheet, there is a temptation to look with a kindly eye on your elderly accounts receivable. If you are trying to hold down your income tax, you will feel an urge to write off slow accounts ruthlessly. It is too bad you cannot have it both ways.

If you keep your books on a cash basis no bad debts will appear, because you only recognize sales when the cash comes in. If it doesn't come in your uncollected accounts may quietly sink out of sight.

The adjusting entry for this situation is:

Dr. Bad debts expense   xxxx

    Cr. Sales   xxxx

to record bad debts for the year ended December 31, 19-

On the face of it this may look a bit silly, but it is advisable to show your bad debts because,

    (a) your sales figure should represent true sales and not sales net of bad debts, and

(b) the net figure would distort your gross profit percentage (see chapter 13, section **b.**).

If you are keeping your books on an accrual basis there are two ways to deal with doubtful accounts. The first is as follows:

Dr. Bad debts expense   xxxx

 Cr. Reserve for bad debts   xxxx

to set up reserve for estimated unrecoverable accounts as at December 31, 19-

This leaves the doubtful accounts sitting in the receivables ledger and subject to your regular collection routine:

The second way is like this:

Dr. Bad debts expense   xxxx

 Cr. Accounts receivable   xxxx

to write off as uncollectible accounts as under:

Company A	xxx
Company B	xxx
Company C	<u>xxx</u>
	<u>xxxx</u>

The second way is perhaps cleaner, but you may find "out of sight, out of mind," and forget to apply the pressures which would normally extract some money from your delinquent debtor.

If you use the first method and have set up a reserve account in the general ledger, when you finally do decide some accounts are worthless, the entry is as follows:

Dr. Bad debts reserve   xxxx

 Cr. Accounts receivable   xxxx

100% uncollectible:

Company A	xxx
Company B	xxx
Company C	<u>xxx</u>
	<u>xxxx</u>

which is logical, because if the accounts are dead then you no longer need to provide for them.

Don't forget that when you make the credit entry or entries in the receivables control account, you *must* make the same entry or entries in the accounts receivable ledger, or vice versa.

Almost all bookkeepers put a tick or a check-mark of some kind alongside the journal figures when they post an entry, so with the above entries there should be *two* ticks alongside the receivables figure, one for the control account posting and the other to indicate the subsidiary ledger has also been posted.

8. Taxes

If you own the building you occupy you will have to pay property taxes. If you paid them at the start of the year you probably debited Deferred Charges. Now you're taking off a monthly statement and you want to charge up to $1/12$th as an expense. You do it like this:

Dr. Property tax expense xxxx

    Cr. Deferred charges xxxx

to apply proportionate property taxes for the month of April, 19-

If you don't have to pay your taxes until the middle of the year or later, then your monthly entry for the first half of the year is slightly different:

Dr. Property Taxes expense xxxx

    Cr. Accrued property taxes xxxx

to set up liability for $1/12$th of estimated taxes for the year

9. Leased space

If you sublet space and your tenant falls behind it should go on your books as an account receivable. However, if and when at the time your tenant signed the lease he or she paid the last three months in advance, remember you haven't earned the money yet, so it should appear on your books as a liability:

Dr. Cash   xxxx

    Cr. Lease prepaid   xxxx

payment for last three months of lease for three years ending December 31, 19-

The latter account is known as a Deferred Credit and you can open a general ledger account under that heading, because you will likely have similar items in the future.

10. Catalogues

If you assemble and publish a sales catalogue and expect to use it for five years without a major change, the whole cost should be debited to Deferred Charges and then the applicable portion for each period can be transferred to an expense account:

Dr. Advertising expense   xxxx

    Cr. Deferred charges   xxxx

*pro-rated portion of catalogue expense for the year ended
December 31, 19-*

This type of entry is similar to your insurance expense and applies to all situations where you put out a lump sum expenditure ahead of time. It's just like depreciation only not quite so complicated.

11. Consignments

Occasionally one of your suppliers will have stored consigned stock (merchandise you don't have to pay for until it's sold) in the back of your building. At your statement date you've sold quite a bit of it but haven't been billed yet. Put it through as a purchase:

Dr. Purchases   xxxx

    Cr. XY Company payable   xxxx

*to set up liability for consigned stock sold but not yet billed to us
as at December 31, 19-*

12. Sales discounts

Often a sale is made on the basis of "2%-10 days" or similar terms and the customer takes advantage of the discount. It will have to be picked up and put on the books:

Dr. Sales discount expense   xxxx

 Cr. Accounts receivable   xxxx

to record 2% discount taken by Company A

The above entry should be made only if the discount is occasional or exceptional. If terms of 2/10 are standard billing procedure then the obvious thing to do is put a debit column in one of your columnar journals (or the synoptic) and label it "sales discounts." This will keep all your discounts in one place and you will have one total for the month instead of driblets scattered throughout the general journal.

13. Purchase discounts

This is the reverse of sales discounts. You are offered a discount on a purchase and you decide to take it after you have already entered the face amount of the purchase invoice in your books. The relevant entry would be:

Dr. Accounts payable (Company X) xxxx

 Cr. Purchase discounts   xxxx

to enter discount taken on Company X invoice dated
January 31, 19-

Here again, if taking discounts is something you do frequently, you can set up a purchase discounts credit column in a journal and accumulate a monthly total. If you always take every discount you can save a bit of book work by deducting the discount in advance from the face amount of the invoice before you make the purchase entry.

14. Receivables and payables on an inventory basis

If you are operating your business on a cash basis, then you will not be making changes every month in your accounts receivable and accounts payable. They were set up on the books by your accountant at the end of your last fiscal year.

Consequently, when the time comes for you to make up statements for this year, you have to bring last year's figures up to date. This is done in two steps.

First you have to remove the old figures from the books by reversing the entry made the previous year:

Dr. Sales   xxxx

    Cr. Accounts receivable   xxxx

to reverse December 31, 19- entry setting up receivables at that date

You have to do this because, being on a cash basis, you have rung up or written down as sales all the money you took in during the past year, including the amounts set up as receivable and counted in as sales in the previous year. You have to eliminate this duplication.

The next step is to enter the current figures, likes this:

Dr. Accounts receivable   xxxx

    Cr. Sales   xxxx

to set up customer accounts outstanding as at December 31, 19-

Sometimes you will find this system referred to as "keeping receivables on an inventory basis." It is an accurate description because you are treating your receivables just as if they were merchandise to be counted at the end of each year. The difference is that a change in your merchandise inventory is reflected in your cost-of-goods-sold, whereas a change in your receivables is reflected in your sales total.

The payables year-end entry is a little longer but is governed by the same principle. All the accounts payable set up on the books at your last year-end were charged by you this year (when you wrote the cheques) to each of the applicable expense accounts. If no adjustments were made it would mean that each expense was debited twice — once when the account was set up and again when you paid it. So you have to reverse last year's entry, like this:

Dr. Accounts payable $2 354.00
   Cr. Purchases $2 051.00
      Accounting   75.00
      Advertising   33.00
      Light and power   45.00
      Repairs and maintenance   61.00
      Supplies and paper   89.00

to reverse accounts payable set up as at December 31, 19-

Having cleared away the previous year's figures you are now ready to make this year's entry, so:

Dr. Purchases $1 824.00
   Accounting   90.00
   Advertising   25.00
   Light and power   25.00
   Repairs and maintenance   160.00
   Supplies and paper   96.00
   Cr. Accounts payable $2 235.00

to record accounts payable as at December 31, 19-

15.   Dividends

If you are operating as a corporation, there will be times when it may cost you less in taxes to pay yourself a dividend rather than an increase in salary. The journal entry is:

Dr. Earned surplus   xxxx
   Cr. Dividends payable   xxxx

Dividend No. 4, payable on January 31, 19- to shareholders of record as of January 10, 190

This should be backed up by the appropriate minutes of a directors' meeting. You can write cheques immediately for the dividend or you can transfer the amounts to shareholders' credit balances in the general ledger, like this:

Dr. Dividends payable   xxxx
   Cr. Shareholder A   xxxx
      Shareholder B   xxxx
      Shareholder C   xxxx

Dividend No. 4 credited to shareholder accounts

The shareholders' balances, if still on the books and still in credit at your year-end, should be shown separately on the company balance sheet as Shareholder Advances. Conversely, if any shareholders owe the company money at your year-end, the amounts should appear in the current assets section of Loans to Shareholders.

16. Income tax

If you operate as a corporation, you must show the company's liability for income tax on your year-end balance sheet. This will necessarily be an estimate because the tax department can be counted on to make some kind of interest or other minor charge, but it should be a close estimate. As mentioned several times in this book you should leave the details of income tax to your accountant, but there is nothing to stop you from making an interim calculation to the near 200 or 300 dollars and using that as a working figure.

The entry setting up your estimated tax liability would be:

Dr. Income tax expense xxxx

Cr. Reserve (or provision) for income tax xxxx
to provide for estimated tax for the year ended December 31, 19-

Some accountants favor debiting Surplus Account rather than Income Tax Expense. The net result is exactly the same because all expense debits end up as a whittling away of the company's retained earnings. However, the first way is more generally used because you can then close out income tax just like any other expense (except that it doesn't reduce your income for tax purposes).

17. Tax instalments

If you are sending in current income tax instalments, you charge them to the reserve for income tax account in the general ledger. If they are monthly and you are not bothering with tax as a monthly expense, this will build up a debit balance in the account. That's quite all right because until your company's liability for tax is determined, so far as you are concerned you are lending the government money.

When you know (or your accountant says *he* knows) the company's tax bill for the year the amount in the reserve will be either more or less than the final estimate.

If the reserve is short of tax, then you need an entry debiting tax expense and crediting the tax reserve to bring it up to what it should be. If your reserve is greater than the tax, then the government, according to your calculations, owes you money and you can classify the amount owed as one of your current assets.

If it's the latter and you continue to make money, you'll probably never see it, because it will be carried forward against next year's tax liability. However, if you have a loss year you'll get a refund as soon as the company's assessment is finalized.

I'm sure you will encounter all of the journal entries mentioned so far and, furthermore, you will have to think up quite a few extra ones for special occasions. You will also have to decide whether entries should be made monthly or whether they can be left for longer periods without inconvenience.

As long as your debits equal your credits you really can't go wrong. If you have second thoughts and want to cancel an entry it's very simple, like this:

Dr. X account   xxxx

    Cr. Y account   xxxx

to reverse entry of January 31, 19-

You don't have to put in any reason for the reversal if you don't feel like it.

However, by the time you have reached this point, you should be brimful of self-confidence, ready to wade right into any bookkeeping situation and to reduce it to its elementary debits and credits.

16
THE TRIAL BALANCE

Let's now take another look at the mainstay of your records, the general ledger.

a. BALANCE SHEET ORDER

If you assembled the pages of the ledger yourself, you probably put them in alphabetical order which, strange as it may seem, is not a good thing. If your accountant assembled the pages he will have put them in "balance sheet order."

There are two reasons for maintaining the ledger in balance sheet order. The first is because many accounts have several different names and somebody not familiar with your system will be confused and waste time.

The second reason is because it is a lot easier to take off financial statements, interim or otherwise, if the ledger accounts are in balance sheet order and statement sequence.

If you're not sure what balance sheet order is, take a look at chapter 13 and refresh your memory. It means the balance sheet and income statement shown thereon were taken from a ledger which was sectioned like this:

Front —   Current assets
           Fixed assets and depreciation reserves
           Prepayments
           Goodwill and other intangibles
           Current liabilities
           Fixed (long-term) liabilities

Middle — Capital
          Drawings (if a proprietorship)
          Surplus (if a corporation)
Back —   Revenue
          Expenses (in alphabetical order)

Once you get used to this arrangement you will find it far more convenient than any alphabetical listing.

b. BALANCING THE GENERAL LEDGER

"To trial balance" is a phrase you will often see in advertisements for bookkeepers in the help-wanted columns of the newspapers. It means the advertiser wants somebody who is capable of writing up the books and balancing them at the end of the month, but not necessarily skilled enough to go further.

Taking off a trial balance is no more complicated than any other bit of arithmetic. You may feel you should write out and add up two parallel columns, one for debit balances and the other for credit balances, but unless you are keeping a "trial balance book," it is not necessary.

Assuming your adding machine contains a subtract bar, you can list both kinds of balances simultaneously. You punch the add bar for the debits and the subtract bar for the credits (or vice versa if you're used to doing it that way — but stick to the same way every time). The minus symbol on the tape will distinguish one kind of balance from the other.

The advantage of having a single listing is that when you press the total key and you get the star, meaning zero, at the bottom of the column of figures, then you know the ledger is in balance. If it is *not* in balance, then the difference is immediately visible.

It is a safe bet that for a while your trial balance tapes are going to end up showing a difference. If there's no difference, then you have achieved your first "sight balance," and you may pat yourself on the back.

Differences are a fact of bookkeeping life and you shouldn't feel discouraged when the tape shows a big difference, because the bigger the difference the easier it is to find. In fact, as you become more proficient in dealing with figures, eventually the prospect of hunting down a difference will be nothing more than a temporary nuisance.

However, before you reach that happy frame of mind you are going to chase down more than one difference and you will have to learn by doing.

Pull your tape out of the machine and be sure to leave five or six inches of blank tape at the bottom because that's where you are going to make the corrections on the tape total. To see how this is done, take a look at Sample #25. The pen alterations on the tape are coded with numbers so you can look back at any time to re-check the figures.

Locating the difference in a general ledger is a process of gradual elimination and, to help you out, here are some of the steps that I have evolved over the year.

(a) Be sure you printed a star, T, zero or other symbol at the head of your column to indicate the machine had been cleared before you started to list.

(b) Check the accuracy of your take-down, watching for nines that could be read as sevens and threes that resemble fives.

(c) Check the column totals in the journals for correct posting to the ledger and do the same thing for the individual items in the general ledger columns in the journals.

(d) Give the journal totals a quick check to be sure they cross-balance.

TRIAL BALANCE TAPES

		Trial ✳ Balance as taken down	Corrected ✳ Trial Balance
		*	*
		349.60-	349.60-
		800.00-	800.00-
(1)	*9063.42*	9 036.42-	9 063.42-
		619.40	619.40
		3 275.63-	3 275.63-
		1 076.50	1 076.50
		380.00	380.00
(2)		2⁷8 931.78-	27 931.78-
		12 920.65-	12 920.65
(3)		435⁸.90	438.90
		2 096.33	2 096.33
		1 289.74	1 289.74
(4)	*8166.00*	81.66	8 166.00
		2 089.32	2 089.32
		57 612.50	57 612.50
(5)		14 83⁷8.21-	14 837.21-
		650.00-	650.00-
		3 940.40-	3 940.40-
		9 059.34-*	*

	(1)	*27.00*
Dr. Over		*9 086.34*
	(2)	*1 000.00*
Dr. Over		*8 086.34*
	(3)	*3.00*
Dr. Over		*8 083.34*
	(4)	*8 084.34*
Cr. Over		*1.00*
	(5)	*1.00*
		0

(e) If any general journal entries are more than two lines make sure total debits equal total credits.

(f) Be sure that all balances at the bottom of completed pages have been carried forward.

(g) Look over last month's trial balance just to be sure there are no alterations on it which should also have been made in the ledger.

(h) Take a colored pencil and tick each entry, both in the ledger and the journals. When you've finished, look for any unticked items in either. (You don't have to make enormous ticks or check-marks — a small dot is sufficient.)

(i) If the difference is divisible by nine it is usually from transposed figures (e.g. — 63 for 36, or 28 for 82). If the difference is 1, 10, 100, or 1 000 it is likely an error in addition or subtraction.

(j) Put the tapes of the current month and last month's balance side by side. A lot of figures won't have changed, but pay attention to the ones which show big changes and run a brief check on them in the ledger.

(k) Try dividing your difference by two and see if the resulting figure is on your tape. If it is it means you have listed a debit as a credit or vice versa.

If none of the above seems to work I suggest you put the books aside and sleep on your difference. Not only will you be fresher in the morning, but it is extraordinary how your subconscious mind seems to work on the problem during the night. Many a time you will spot your differences as soon as you open the ledger and you'll wonder how you ever managed to miss it the day before.

But no matter what you do, don't give up. You know there is an obvious error lurking somewhere among those

189

figures, and you also know you are quite capable of finding it.

Never let any set of books get the better of you!

c. CLOSING THE GENERAL LEDGER

So you've made all the year-end adjustments, the general ledger is in balance and you're feeling pretty good about the whole affair. (If you're afraid of losing your tape you can start a "trial balances book" and write in all the accounts and amounts every time you balance the ledger.)

You are about to wind up one fiscal period and launch another, so the first thing on the agenda is to clear out all the revenue and expense figures for the expired period and then transfer the difference, which is either a profit or a loss, to your capital account, or, if you are a corporation, to your earned surplus or retained earnings account.

The asset and liability figures are not affected at all. They are exactly the same on the first day of your new period as they were on the last day of your old period.

And now, because it's easier to work with actual figures rather than a collection of x's, we're going to use Joe Spiff's little business to demonstrate.

If you turn back to Sample #23, you'll note that Joe started out his fiscal year with a merchandise inventory worth $7 306, but by the end of the year it was down to $6 469, a decrease of $837.

This is important, because Joe's accountant must make one final adjustment before he can get down to the actual closing of the operating accounts. This is the journal entry he made after he was given the closing inventory figure:

Dr. Trading account	7 306.00	
Cr.(old) inventory, Dec. 31, 19-		7 306.00
Dr.(new) inventory, Dec. 31, 19-	6 469.00	
Cr. Trading account		6 469.00

to remove opening inventory from books and enter closing inventory

Trading Account is a convenience account used only at the year-end and it reflects the difference, plus or minus, between the starting and ending inventories. In this case there is $837 drop in value and that is just as much an expense as any other debit balance in the expense section of the books.

Sample #26 shows the trial balance right after Joe's accountant has made the above journal entry.

Now, hold your breath and we'll put through the closing entries:

Dr. Sales	102 910.00	
Cr. Purchases		76 551.00
Accounting		600.00
Advertising		328.00
Bad debts		100.00
Delivery		417.00
Insurance		255.00
Laundry		238.00
Licences and permits		140.00
Light & power		456.00
Miscellaneous		221.00
Mortgage interest		226.00
Payroll & other taxes		655.00
Rent		960.00
Repairs & maintenance		683.00
Stationery & stamps		142.00
Supplies and paper		875.00
Taxes		842.00
Wages		6 936.00
Depreciation — building		1 200.00
— truck		300.00
— furn. & fixtures		97.00
Trading account		837.00
J. Spiff, capital		9 851.00

to close the operating accounts to capital for the year ended December 31, 19-

SAMPLE #26
TRIAL BALANCE

J. SPIFF & COMPANY
Trial Balance as at December 31, 19—
(before closing)

	Dr.	Cr.
Cash on hand	200	
Cash in bank	1 593	
Accounts receivable	4 381	
Reserve for bad debts		650
Inventory, December 31, 19—	6 469	
Utility deposit	75	
Building	24 000	
Building res. for depreciation		3 600
Truck	1 200	
Truck res. for depreciation		300
Furniture & fixtures	975	
Furniture & fixtures res. for depreciation		292
Land	5 000	
Deferred charges	258	
Goodwill	500	
Bank loan		1 500
Accounts payable		2 235
Sundry creditors		327
Sales tax payable		98
Mortgage payable		1 750
Capital		32 048
Drawings	8 000	
Sales		102 910
Purchases	76 551	
Accounting	600	
Advertising	328	
Bad debts	100	
Delivery	417	
Insurance	255	
Laundry	238	
Licenses & permits	140	
Light & power	456	
Miscellaneous	221	
Mortgage interest	226	
Payroll & other taxes	655	
Rent	960	
Repairs & maintenance	683	
Stationery & stamps	142	
Supplies & paper	875	
Taxes	842	
Wages	6 936	
Depreciation — Building	1 200	
— Truck	300	
— Furniture & fixtures	97	
Trading account	837	
	145 710	145 710

192

The one entry remaining to clear away the debris from last year relates to Joe's drawing account. It's closed out like this:

Dr. J. Spiff, capital   8 000.00
    Cr. J. Spiff, drawing account   8 000.00
to close Mr. Spiff's drawing account for the year 19-

After the above entry had gone through Joe's accountant took off another trial balance from the ledger, shown in Sample #27.

The only difference between this trial balance and the balance sheet in Sample #22 is that the latter is more readable. If you want to write out your own balance sheet from the trial balance after closing, the only thing you have to watch is the capital section. This should show last year's closing figure, increased by this year's profit and decreased by this year's drawings, thereby arriving at the final figure for the current year.

If you're writing out your income statement you'll find it equally straightforward. The only place where you have to be careful is in the costs-of-goods-sold section, where it is customary to show the year's opening inventory, plus purchases, less closing inventory rather than the single trading account figure in your trial balance before closing.

d. THE "INSTANT" PROFIT AND LOSS STATEMENT

Before we leave the subject, let us have a quick look at another use for your trial balance. If you don't mind writing out the account names as well as the figures, you can set it up so that it will give you your *unadjusted* profit (or loss) to date with an absolute minimum of bookkeeping.

Because your accounts are in balance sheet order (if they aren't, they should be,) there is what you might call a natural dividing line between the assets/liabilities/capital sections and the revenue/expense sections. Thanks to this sequence

J. SPIFF & COMPANY
Trial Balance after Closing
December 31, 19—

	Dr.	Cr.
Cash on hand	200	
Cash in bank	1 593	
Accounts receivable	4 381	
Reserve for bad debts		650
Merchandise inventory	6 469	
Utility deposit	75	
Building	24 000	
Building res. for depreciation		3 600
Truck	1 200	
Truck res. for depreciation		300
Furniture & fixtures	975	
Furniture & fixtures res. for depreciation		292
Land	5 000	
Deferred charges	258	
Goodwill	500	
Bank loan		1 500
Accounts payable		2 235
Sundry creditors		327
Sales tax payable		98
Mortgage payable		1 750
Capital, J. Spiff		33 899
	44 651	44 651

it is possible to get a fast approximation of what's happened in your business up to the trial balance date.

To do this you take an adding machine tape of your assets and drawings on the one side of your trial balance and then a tape of your liabilities and capital on the other. If the asset-and-drawings total is the larger of the two, then the difference is profit. If the liabilities-and-capital is the larger, then the difference is loss. (See Sample #28.)

It should be emphasized that this is a rough calculation, because it doesn't take into account depreciation or inventory changes and, if you are on a cash basis, increases or decreases in receivables or payables. Nevertheless, when these last three variables are relatively stable from month to month and if you will remember you haven't included depreciation, it will give you a useful answer.

As a check on your arithmetic, when you write out your figures leave four blank lines after the assets/drawings section and then fill in the balancing figure in the right-hand column and call it Unadjusted Profit. (It goes in the left-hand column if it's a loss.) Then draw a single line across both columns, fill in the totals and draw a double line across the page.

Now put the same profit figure at the bottom of the expense figures in the lower left-hand column and call it profit as above. Draw a single line under the two lower columns, add them up, and once more you have that pleasing sight, two equal totals side by side.

Sample #26, which consists of Joe Spiff's trial balance *before* his year-end closing adjustments, show a profit of $13 115. This is $3 264 more than that shown in his formal year-end statement, but if you subtract the $837 inventory decrease and the $1 597 for depreciation you are left with an unadjusted profit of $10 681. True, this is 10% more than the final figure, but during the year the results are close enough for Joe to know he is on the right track.

SAMPLE #28
PROFIT AND LOSS STATEMENT

J. SPIFF & COMPANY
"Instant" Profit & Loss Statement
Trial Balance (unadjusted)
as at Dec. 31, 19—

	Dr.	Cr.
Cash	200	
Bank	1 593	
Accounts receivable	4 381	
Reserve for bad debts		550
Inventory	7 306	
Utility deposit	75	
Building	24 000	
Building reserve for depreciation		2 400
Truck	1 200	
Furniture & fixtures	975	
Furniture & fixtures res. for depreciation		195
Land	5 000	
Deferred charges	587	
Goodwill	500	
Bank loan		1 500
Accounts payable		2 235
Sundry creditors		152
Sales tax payable		98
Mortgage payable		1 524
Capital		32 048
Drawings	8 000	
Subtotals	53 817	40 702
Unadjusted profit		13 115
	53 817	53 817
Sales		102 910
Purchases	76 551	
Accounting	600	
Advertising	128	
Delivery	417	
Insurance	126	
Laundry	238	
Licenses & permits	140	
Light & power	456	
Miscellaneous	221	
Payroll taxes	655	
Rent	960	
Repairs & maintenance	683	
Stationery & stamps	142	
Supplies & paper	875	
Taxes on property	842	
Wages	6 761	
Subtotal	89 795	
Profit as above	13 115	
	102 910	102 910

17

THE COLUMNAR WORK SHEET

The closing adjustments for the average business are preceded by a lot of mulling over things like the bad debts estimate, inventory valuation, management salaries, depreciation and so on. To minimize the delay caused by all this fuss and feathers and to permit them to get ahead with a set of preliminary statements, accountants invented an ingenious arrangement called the columnar work sheet. This device enables the accountant to keep all the adjustments afloat on a tentative basis until the final decisions are made. It also enables him to confine all his journalizing to a working paper, rather than making entries in the general journal and then having to change them.

To show you what this is all about I will ask you now to assume the role of Joe Spiff's accountant as he gets ready to make up the columnar work sheet illustrated in Sample #29.

First, you will need to pick up at the stationery store a wide columnar pad, at least 8 figure-columns wide, or better still, 10 or 12 figure-columns plus a description column. It should be at least 45 lines deep. You'll also need a 2-column pad, 45 lines or more deep, which will serve as your general journal in padded form.

For the sake of clarity let us do the whole thing by numbered steps.

Step 1. You start by writing out your unadjusted trial balance as at December, 19-, complete with account titles, in columns 1 and 2 on the left-hand side of the sheet. Because you are going to run into some accounts that are used only at

SAMPLE #29
COLUMNAR WORK SHEET

	1.	2.	3.	4.	5.

ACCOUNT NAME	Unadjusted Trial Balance		Journal Entry No.	Journal Entries	
	Dr.	Cr.		Dr.	Cr.
Cash on hand	200				
Cash in bank	1 593				
Accounts receivable	4 381				
Reserve for bad debts		550	(1)		100
Inventory	7 306		(2)	6 469	7 306
Utility Deposit	75				
Building	24 000				
Building, res. for depreciation		2,400	(3)		1 200
Truck	1 200				
Truck, res. for depreciation			(3)		300
Furn. & fixtures	975				
Furn. & fixtures, res. for depreciation		195	(3)		97
Land	5 000				
Deferred charges	587		(6)		200
			(4)		129
Goodwill	500				
Bank loan		1 500			
Accounts payable		2 235			
Sundry creditors		152	(7)		175
Sales tax payable		98			
Mortgage payable		1 524	(5)		226
Capital		32 048			
Drawings	8 000				
Sales		102 910			
Purchases	76 551				
Accounting	600				
Advertising	128		(6)	200	
Bad debts			(1)	100	
Delivery	417				
Insurance	126		(4)	129	
Laundry	238				
Licenses & permits	140				
Light & power	456				
Miscellaneous	221				
Mortgage interest			(5)	226	
Payroll & other taxes	655				
Rent	960				
Repairs & maintenance	683				
Stationery & stamps	142				
Supplies & paper	875				
Property taxes	842				
Wages	6 761		(7)	175	
Depreciation			(3)	1 597	
Trading Account			(2)	7 306	6 469

198

SAMPLE #29 — Continued

6.		7.	8.	9.	10.
Adjusted Trial Balance		Income Statement		Balance Sheet	
Dr.	Cr.	Dr.	Cr.	Dr.	Cr.
200				200	
1 593				1 593	
4 381				4 381	
	650				650
6 469				6 469	
75				75	
24 000				24 000	
	3 600				3 600
1 200				1 200	
	300				300
975				975	
	292				292
5 000				5 000	
258				258	
500				500	
	1 500				1 500
	2 235				2 235
	327				327
	98				98
	1 750				1 750
	32 048				32 048
8 000				8 000	
	102 910		102 910		
76 551		76 551			
600		600			
328		328			
100		100			
417		417			
255		255			
238		238			
140		140			
456		456			
221		221			
226		226			
655		655			
960		960			
683		683			
142		142			
875		875			
842		842			
6 936		6 936			
1 597		1 597			
837		837			
(Subtotals)		93 059	102 910	52 651	42 800
		9 851			9 851
		102 910	102 910	52 651	52 651

year-end, such as the Trading account, you leave space for them in the form of a blank line every so often.

Step 2. You number your adjusting entries and write them out on your two-column pad, as illustrated in Sample #30.

Step 3. You put Journal Entries, Dr. and Cr. at the head of columns 3 and 4 and enter therein, opposite the trial balance accounts, all the journal entries you have written out on your pad.

At this point I would like to caution you. All through this book whenever a ledger entry has been illustrated it has been made down the page, from one line to the next. If you've been posting the ledger yourself you will have done this hundreds of times.

Now you have to break yourself of this habit temporarily and *think horizontally, because all the entries on your work sheet are across the page* and not down the page.

Step 4. You head up columns 5 and 6 with Adjusted Trial Balance, Dr. and Cr. You take each unadjusted figure in columns 1 and 2 and extend it horizontally, picking up any debits and credits in columns 3 and 4 as you go and ending up with the adjusted figures in columns 5 and 6.

Step 5. At this stage as a safeguard you add up each set of twin columns to make sure they balance.

Step 6. You're getting close to the pay-off. You head up columns 7 and 8 with Income Statement, Dr. and Cr., and columns 9 and 10 with Balance Sheet, Dr. and Cr. You extend all the asset, liability and capital figures into the Balance Sheet columns and all the revenue and expense figures into the Income Statement columns.

Step 7. You add up each of columns 7, 8, 9, and 10 and write in the amounts as subtotals. Check your arithmetic by adding the debit subtotals in columns 7 and 9 and the credit subtotals in columns 8 and 10. The two figures are equal.

SAMPLE #30
ADJUSTING JOURNAL ENTRIES

1. Dr. Bad debts expense   100
   Cr. Reserve for bad debts   100
   to set up estimated reserve for
   the period

2. Dr. Trading account   7 306
   Cr. Old inventory   7 306

   Dr. New inventory   6 469
   Cr. Trading account   6 469
   to remove opening inventory from
   the books and to enter closing
   inventory

3. Dr. Depreciation expense   1 597
   Cr. Res. for Dep'n, Bldg.   1 200
       "   "   "   Truck   300
       "   "   "   Furn & Fixt.   97
   to record depreciation for
   the period

4. Dr. Insurance expense   129
   Cr. Deferred Charges   129
   to record insurance expired during
   the period

5. Dr. Interest expense   226
   Cr. Mortgage payable   226
   to record interest accrued
   during the period

6. Dr. Advertising expense   200
   Cr. Deferred Charges   200
   to record catalogue cost amortized
   during the period

7. Dr. Wages   175
   Cr. Sundry creditors   175
   to record wages accrued and unpaid
   at statement date

Step 8. The difference between columns 7 and 8 is your profit and it is the same as the difference between columns 9 and 10. For a tidy bottom line you write in the difference under the column 7 and 10 subtotals and add the two together. This produces two sets of identical figures, side by side, which to an accountant signifies all's well with the world.

At the risk of introducing a discordant note, if the subtotal of column 7 is greater than that of column 8, then you have incurred a loss. If it's any consolation you can still balance up by shifting the difference to columns 8 and 9.

If your business is ever audited by an outside firm they will make up a columnar work sheet for their own use. As auditors, after consultation with you, they will calculate all the final adjusting entries and present them to your bookkeeper or accountant in typewritten form. He or she can then staple or paste the sheets into the synoptic or the general journal and post directly from them to the general ledger accounts. The auditors will also furnish a memo showing what the balances in Capital and Surplus accounts should be after all the year-end dust settles. In due course they will provide you with a half a dozen sets of financial statements, each one done up in a colored cover and tied together with an artistic bit of ribbon. A bit later you will receive an artistic bill.

But to descend from the heights inhabited by auditors to the everyday world of Joe Spiff, sometimes in the middle of the year and perhaps in the middle of your busiest season, your bank may demand a full-dress set of financial statements.

This is where the columnar work sheet is invaluable. You can lay out all your information systematically and extract the desired information cleanly. You don't have to fill the general journal and the general ledger with a jungle of adjusting entries just to accommodate your bank manager.

As you become more at home on the work sheet you can even eliminate the adjusted trial balance columns and leap across from the journal entries to the statement columns.

By the time you get to this stage you should consider yourself a competent bookkeeper and be able to hold your own in any discussion with your accountant — even if he does have a set of initials after his name.

You may want to go further into the art of accountancy. You may discover there is a fascination in marshalling squads of figures and drilling them into good behavior.

Many years ago I remember hearing about a young man who studied algebra and who was moved to tears by the beauty of the binomial theorem. I doubt if anybody has been similarly affected by a profit and loss statement, but every accountant will know what I mean when I say a well-constructed balance sheet can give its architect deep emotional satisfaction.

If you want to go further into accountancy you will find a lot of people willing to help you. Why, one day you might end up by writing a book on the subject!

18

"THE APPLE-BOX SITUATION"

Sometimes, despite the best of intentions, you get behind with your books. And by "behind" I don't mean a month or two — I mean the stuff piles up in file cases, boxes and bundles until every time you look at it you wonder how one small business could result in enough paper for a fair-sized salvage drive.

We won't go into the reasons why you are behind with your records. They can be, and often are, quite good ones. Suffice it that the mess has got to be unscrambled, and somewhere along the line you will have to call in an accountant.

How much is it going to cost?

That depends on whether you are going to dump the whole thing into your accountant's hands "as is," or whether you are willing to do some of the preliminary sorting and classifying yourself.

IF THE FORMER, your accountant will class the job as "an apple-box proposition" (so called because that is often the container in which "the books" reach the office), and he will hesitate to quote a fee in advance. Or if he does quote one, it will be a round figure containing a liberal allowance for unforeseen snags.

IF THE LATTER, you will no longer be an "apple-box" client. You will be a client who has "a certain amount of back work to be done," which is a vastly different proposition.

So, in the event that you want to keep the fee down, here are the things to do, accompanied by a list of "don'ts" and the reasons therefore.

(a) Read through this manual from cover to cover. You don't have to study it, or even read slowly, but read it. By doing so you will unconsciously acquire an "accounting point of view" which in turn will be reflected in your subsequent classifying and sorting operations.

(b) BANK STATEMENTS AND CANCELLED CHEQUES: Make sure you have the bank statement and cheques for every month. Leave the cheques exactly as they came from the bank. Don't sort them into numerical order under the impression it will help — because it won't. And don't take out any cheques or bank debit memos.

Have the stubs available with the "what for" of each cheque written on each stub. It will also help if you write the "what for" on the face of each cheque, because your accountant may want to save time by ignoring stubs and, except for year-end months, running your cheques through on a "when-paid" basis, rather than "when-issued."

If the bank charged back any NSF cheques, make a note on the bank debit slip whether:

— the cheque was redeposited and collected in due course
— the cheque was redeemed by the maker in cash
— the cheque was completely uncollectible.

(c) LOANS — Give your accountant details of any loans, bank or otherwise, that you received during the year and how much is still owing on them at the year-end.

(d) Make a list, or at least, give your accountant a total figure for your accounts receivable at your year-end.

(e) Make a list of your accounts payable at your year-end, showing *subtotals* for each class of expense they represent, such as purchases, supplies, stationery, advertising, etc.

(f) CASH PAY-OUTS — This is where you can save your accountant a lot of time. Sit down at a table some evening with all your receipted pay-out slips in front of you (*cash* pay-outs, not *cheque* pay-outs).

If you have made some pay-outs without slips, make out memo slips then and there.

Sort all your papers into piles, each pile representing one of the expense accounts that will appear on your income statement. Most of the papers will be in "purchases" pile, which is as it should be.

Now take your adding machine (if you haven't got one, borrow or rent one) and list each pile. Staple each adding machine tape to the pile it goes with (some of them will be too thick and you will have to use rubber bands), and write on the tape under the total the name of the expense it represents.

(g) Don't, if you can possibly avoid it, give your accountant a box full of receipted bills, some of them cash pay-outs and some of them payments made by cheque. Few things will raise his blood pressure quicker than the sight of a box full of receipts, half of them cash receipts, half of them cheque receipts, all mixed together like last year's dead leaves, with no clue as to which is which. And nothing will make him think more quickly of raising his fee.

(h) Figure out your sales for the year, either month by month, or a total for the whole year, so you can give him the figures and say, "Here it is." *Don't*, if you can avoid it, give him a bag of cash register tapes and expect him to unreel them, day by day, and list the

206

daily totals. He'll do it if he has to, but it will certainly cost you money.

(i) If your cash register tape shows pay-outs as well as sales, *don't*, if you can avoid it, make him go through the figures on each day's tape, item by item, day by day, trying to catch all the pay-out figures. Chances are he'd miss a lot of them anyway, and as for the ones he did pick out, he would have to ask you what each and every one of them was for. Oh, yes, I know, the cash register people provide space on the tape beside each pay-out, so you can write in what it is for. But perhaps your accountant can't read your writing. So, to be on the safe side, he will charge such items to you personally, and your business will thereby show more profit than was actually made, with income tax to pay accordingly.

(j) If this is the first time the books have been written up, give your accountant all the information called for in the chapter "On Buying a Business." If you have been in business for some time and this is just a temporary relapse, give him a copy of the last balance sheet you have and also the last income tax return you filed.

(k) If you employ help, give him copies of all government returns accompanying tax deduction and pension plan remittances, etc. In fact, give him copies of any and all government returns you have made during the period he is working on. Give him your payroll book if you have one, and if you haven't, then be sure to give him full details on employee's gross pay, deductions and net pay. If you pay by cheque, write these details on the cheque stub. If you pay by cash, write them on the pay-out slips.

(l) If you have bought any equipment (not for resale), make sure your accountant sees the purchase contract or the invoice you received when you bought it.

If you are buying on time, make sure the contract shows details such as finance charges, registration fees, insurance, interest, etc.

(m) If at any time you put more money into the business, be sure to let your accountant know about it. This is very important from your point of view, because otherwise your investment might end up as part of a sales total.

(n) BANK DEPOSITS: You can include these among your pay-out totals, or you can forget about them and let your accountant list them from your bank statement or passbook. He will list the deposits anyway, but he will be glad to have your figures as a double check.

That pretty well covers the ground work you do. There is, however, one further step to take — it involves a little work, but the result is worth the trouble — and that is, using the figures you have assembled, see if your cash position works out reasonably.

Put your figures in the same sequence as a daily cash sheet, only this time you use the figure for a whole year (or whatever the period that has to be caught up). Thus:

Cash on hand at start		$ 100.00
Plus		
Cash from sales	$80 000.00	
Cash from loans	5 000.00	
Cash from other sources	600.00	85 600.00
Total cash to be accounted for		$85 700.00
Less		
Expense pay-outs	57 000.00	
Cash put in bank	23 700.00	80 700.00
		5 000.00
Less		
Estimated drawings for personal use		4 800.00
Cash on hand		$200.00

If you have a record of your own drawings, you can, if you like, group them with your expense pay-outs and bank deposits instead of subtracting them on the line below. More often, when you let things get behind, you don't keep track of personal drawings, and consequently the only way to arrive at them is to figure they are the cash which should be there but isn't.

It may happen that after you have assembled your year's figures — (we are talking "year" because that is the longest period that can be handled at one go, but it may, of course, be any shorter period) — after you have the final line-up, you may find yourself with a result that is definitely odd.

The first oddity may be that, even after a liberal estimate for drawings, you show far more cash on hand than you actually have.

This may be due to —

> — overstatement of sales due to duplication, arithmetical error, or similar reasons
> — overstatement of cash loans, cash investment or other source of cash, vouchers, bank deposits overlooked, etc.

The second oddity is the reverse of the first. You may end up with a minus quantity of cash on hand. That's to say, your total paid out by way of expenses, bank deposits and drawings exceeds what you received from sales, loans, initial investment, etc.

This is obviously an impossible situation and it has arisen only because —

> — you may have omitted to put down some of your sales, loans, or other sources of cash,
> — you may have duplicated some of your cash pay-outs when listing them,
> — there are arithmetical errors somewhere in your calculations.

In either case it will pay you to go over your figures and find out what's wrong, because any changes your accountant makes will be on the safe side.

That is to say:

(a) If you show more cash on hand than you should, he won't change any sales or expense figures. He'll presume you drew more money out than you remembered, and increase your drawings figures accordingly.

(b) If you show a minus quantity of cash (known as a "credit balance in cash") he will *increase* sales to account for the cash you claim to have paid out.

He won't do either without consulting you first and trying to get to the bottom of your cash mystery. Then, if you can't account for the discrepancy, he will have to make a change along the lines of (a) or (b), for otherwise he would be drawing up a statement which he knew to be wrong, and accountants don't do that kind of thing. At least, not if they want to stay in the accounting business.

Don't expect your accountant to set up an elaborate set of books for your back work. He will compile records adequate for his purpose and adequate for the tax department if they want to see them, but he won't splurge into ledgers, journals and fancy stationery. In fact, the chances are he will write up all your back work on multi-column "spreadsheets" and will rely heavily on adding machine tapes. He is interested in the end statement, not in the means by which that end is attained.

And don't expect your accountant to work for nothing. To unscramble old business details requires a high degree of professional skill, something which can only be acquired after intensive training and experience.

He will not overcharge you. I don't know why it is, but accountants, as a class, are more apt to undercharge than overcharge. So when he presents his bill you can be pretty sure you have got your money's worth.

He will no doubt suggest that now the back work is cleaned up you keep your records up to date in future.

That is sound advice. It may appear to cost you more, per month, to have them written up regularly, but, take it from me, in the long run it will save you money.

If you have enjoyed this book and would like to receive a free catalogue of all Self-Counsel titles, please write to:

Self-Counsel Press
1481 Charlotte Road
North Vancouver, B.C.
V7J 1H1

Or visit us on the World Wide Web at *http://www.self-counsel.com*